# Cambridge Elements ≡

**Elements in Business Strategy**
edited by
J.-C. Spender
*Rutgers Business School*

T0286964

# AGENT-BASED STRATEGIZING

Duncan A. Robertson
*School of Business and Economics, Loughborough University, and St Catherine's College, University of Oxford*

CAMBRIDGE
UNIVERSITY PRESS

## CAMBRIDGE
### UNIVERSITY PRESS

University Printing House, Cambridge CB2 8BS, United Kingdom

One Liberty Plaza, 20th Floor, New York, NY 10006, USA

477 Williamstown Road, Port Melbourne, VIC 3207, Australia

314–321, 3rd Floor, Plot 3, Splendor Forum, Jasola District Centre,
New Delhi – 110025, India

79 Anson Road, #06–04/06, Singapore 079906

Cambridge University Press is part of the University of Cambridge.

It furthers the University's mission by disseminating knowledge in the pursuit of
education, learning, and research at the highest international levels of excellence.

www.cambridge.org
Information on this title: www.cambridge.org/9781108738019
DOI: 10.1017/9781108767835

© Duncan A. Robertson 2019

First published 2019

A catalogue record for this publication is available from the British Library.

ISBN 978-1-108-73801-9 Paperback
ISSN 2515-0693 (online)
ISSN 2515-0685 (print)

# Agent-Based Strategizing

## Elements in Business Strategy

DOI: 10.1017/9781108767835
First published online: July 2019

Duncan A. Robertson
*School of Business and Economics, Loughborough University,
and St Catherine's College, University of Oxford*

**Author for correspondence:** Duncan A. Robertson, d.a.robertson@lboro.ac.uk

**Abstract:** Strategic management is a system of continual disequilibrium, with firms in a continual struggle for competitive advantage and relative fitness. Models that are dynamic in nature are required if we are to really understand the complex notion of sustainable competitive advantage. And new tools are required to tackle challenges of how firms should compete in environments characterized by both exogenous shocks and intense endogenous competition.
A rich history of alternative dynamic models exist in other social and natural sciences, some of which have been incorporated into the strategic management literature, notably the *NK* series of models. Yet there is a whole history of models from systems models, organizational ecology and general fitness landscape models that can be converted to agent-based models and used for the study of strategic management.
Agent-based modelling of firms' strategies offers an alternative analytical approach, where individual firm or component parts of a firm are modelled, each with its own strategy. Where traditional models can assume homogeneity of actors, agent-based models simulate each firm individually. This allows experimentation of strategic moves, which is particularly important where reactions to strategic moves are nontrivial.
This Element introduces agent-based models and their use within management, reviews the influential *NK* suite of models and offers an agenda for the development of agent-based models in strategic management.

**Keywords:** agent-based modelling, strategic management

ISBNs: 9781108738019 (PB), 9781108767835 (OC)
ISSNs: 2515-0693 (online), 2515-0685 (print)

# Contents

Introduction                                                        1

1  Agent-Based Models                                              1

2  Antecedents: the World of Agent-Based Models                   11

3  Into the Strategic Literature                                  18

4  An Agenda for the Future                                       33


   References                                                     38

   Appendix: PRISMA Methodology                                   48

## Introduction

Strategic management, in line with other social science fields, is difficult: it is a subject that does not lend itself easily to experimentation, as the environment co-evolves at the same time that specific strategies are being evaluated. Agent-based modelling offers an exciting opportunity to experiment where interactions between other firms and the complex environment can be modelled and robust strategies developed accordingly.

Agent-based modelling provides an opportunity to experiment by way of simulation, where experiments can be undertaken, strategies evaluated, and interdependencies examined without making irreversible commitments of one's own firm. Agent-based modelling builds on the long history of work within complexity science, where entities – in our case firms – interact in a non-linear manner, much as they do in real life (despite many theorists' simplifying assumptions that assume they do not). Strategic management, when defined as the search to gain and maintain competitive advantage, is starting to be examined by researchers using agent-based modelling techniques borrowed from evolutionary biology, physics and other natural sciences. This offers a fascinating opportunity to extend existing research and to develop new models for competition that are not constrained by the traditional limitations of equilibrium or comparative statics.

We investigate in the following way. Section 1 is a review of agent-based models and of complexity science more generally. Section 2 offers a review of antecedents to the world of agent-based modelling from economic and systems models, organizational ecology, and biological models with their conceptualizations of fitness landscapes. Section 3 introduces the *NK* model, perhaps the most successful agent-based model within strategic management and organizational science, and shows alternative models that include competition between firms, the lack of competition being a limitation of the *NK* series of papers. Finally, Section 4 suggests directions for future research building on existing agent-based models that have yet to be fully developed within the field of strategic management.

## 1 Agent-Based Models

Agent-based models, a class of simulation models (for a general review of simulation, see Robinson 2004), can be traced back to game theorists' research such as von Neumann's (1966) 'work on computers' and later cellular automata such as Conway's *Game of Life* (Gardner 1970). These cellular automata were grid-based simulations whose cells could be in a state of 'on' or 'off'. Simple transition rules changed these states, dependent upon the states of their neighbours, which often resulted in elaborate evolutions of the system. Genetic algorithms have since been used within the strategic management community to 'breed' competitive strategies (Midgley *et al.* 1997).

The birth of agent-based models can be traced back to Schelling (1971a, 1971b) in which a 'general theory of tipping' (Schelling 1978) was developed. Schelling's model showed that if *individuals* (modelled as being on a cellular grid) had even a slight preference of being near neighbours with characteristics similar to themselves, the *system* of individuals would evolve to be segregated. This connection between 'micromotives and macrobehavior' led to a vast range of subsequent models, some of which are discussed later in this Element.

Axelrod (1997:3) describes agent-based modelling as the 'third way' of doing science:

> Agent-based modelling is a third way of doing science. Like deduction, it starts with a set of explicit assumptions. But unlike deduction, it does not prove theorems. Instead a simulation generates data that can be analyzed inductively. Unlike typical induction, however, the simulated data comes from a rigorously specified set of rules rather than direct measurement of the real world. While induction can be used to find patterns in data, and deduction can be used to find consequences of assumptions, simulation modeling can be used to aid intuition.

Bonabeau's (2002:7280) review of agent-based models as a specific method of simulation sums up the methodology quite nicely:

> In agent-based modeling (ABM), a system is modeled as a collection of autonomous decision-making entities called agents. Each agent individually assesses its situation and makes decisions on the basis of a set of rules. Agents may execute various behaviors appropriate for the system they represent – for example, producing, consuming, or selling. Repetitive competitive interactions between agents are a feature of agent-based modeling, which relies on the power of computers to explore dynamics out of the reach of pure mathematical methods.

Bonabeau goes on to describe agent-based modelling as a 'mindset more than a technology' – the fact that a system can be *conceptualized* as a group of interacting actors or agents, be these individuals within an organization or firms interacting with other firms in an industry. For Epstein (Epstein and Axtell 1996; Epstein 1999), agent-based models are 'generative' models, 'growing' societies from the bottom up.

Agent-based modelling has also been used to introduce models that are actually cellular automata models (Goldenberg *et al.* 2010) with the ensuing limitations on topology. For a discussion on the similarities and distinctions between such modelling frameworks, see Robertson (2019), and for a more general introduction to agent-based modelling, see Gilbert (2008), North and Macal (2007), Gilbert and Troitzch (2005), Axelrod and Tesfatsion (2006), Woodridge and Jennings (1995) and Robertson and Caldart (2009). A primer on agent-based modelling is given in the following subsection.

## 1.1 Agent-Based Modelling: a Primer

Agent-based models, also called individual-based models, are a class of computer simulations where individual components of a system are modelled so that the collective behavior of those agents comprises the behavior of the system as a whole. As an exemplar of agent-based modelling, we review a classic agent-based model, Schelling's (1969, 1971a) 'Model of Segregation'.

Schelling observed that individuals are segregated according to various attributes such as gender, race, income, language, and other classes. While some of this can be explained by the work of a central planner imposing choices on individuals, an alternative explanation exists – that the micro-level behaviour of individuals within the system generates the macro-level system behaviour, in this case the segregation of individuals.

Consider a system of *N* individuals, of two types. In this example, we can visualize these by supporters of political parties, the light greys and the dark greys. For reasons of modelling simplicity, these individuals are assumed to be arranged in a grid, although this assumption is not required for the segregation behaviour to manifest itself. One can visualize this system as agents of two types representing the agents' political affiliation: dark grey or light grey, as shown in Figure 1. These *N* individuals are distributed randomly in the grid.

These individuals or 'agents' have a limited knowledge of the world: they can observe the political affiliation of their neighbours, but not the political affiliation of all individuals in the system. In this way, they are 'intendedly rational, but boundedly so' (Simon 1997:88) – that is to say, the individual's behavior is 'subjectively rational if it maximizes attainment relative to the actual knowledge of the subject' (Simon 1947:76).

The behavior of individuals is as follows:

• Each individual observes their neighbours and calculates whether the individual is in a local minority. In the example in Figure 1(b), the dark grey individual at the centre of the large square is in a local minority, as only one out of six neighbours are of the same political affiliation (in numerical terms, $1/6 \approx 17\% < 50\%$). If the proportion of neighbours with the same political affiliation is less than 50 per cent, the individual is 'unhappy', and if this proportion is 50 per cent or above, the individual is 'happy'.

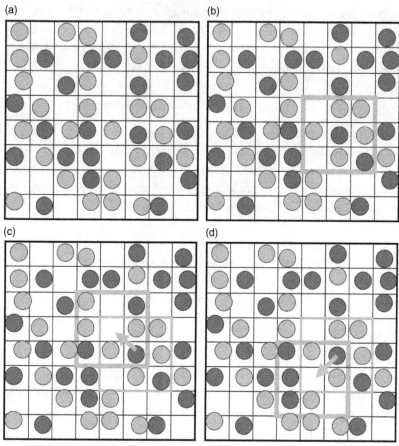

**Figure 1** Movement of unhappy dark grey agent showing candidate locations

- Unhappy individuals look for a vacant location where they will be happy. In Figure 1(c), the dark grey individual tests to see whether they would be happy in the location to their north-west. In this case, they would have two out of six neighbours ($2/6 \approx 33\% < 50\%$) with the same political affiliation as their own, which means that, in this location, they would remain unhappy, and this location is not viable.
- This search continues until an individual finds a location where they are happy. In Figure 1(d), the dark grey individual investigates the location to their south-west. In this location, they will have three out of six neighbours with the same political affiliation ($3/6 = 50\% \geq 50\%$), and this individual is happy. They remain at this location.

In each round, some individuals change their state from happy to unhappy, others change their state from unhappy to happy and others remain either happy or unhappy. The model continues until all individuals are happy and equilibrium is established.

The remarkable thing about this model, over and above the micro-level actions causing the macro-level behavior of the system, is that there arises a counter-intuitive result: individuals do not have to desire to be in a local majority in order for segregation to take place.

Consider the initial conditions shown in Figure 2(a), where dark grey and light grey individuals are randomly allocated to locations within a grid. These individuals possess the same threshold of happiness, $\sigma$, defined as the ratio of similar neighbours to total neighbours, in this case, 50 per cent. Some of these individuals will be initially happy (denoted by happy faces) or unhappy (denoted by sad faces). The model is allowed to run, with unhappy individuals moving locations, until an equilibrium is reached where all individuals are happy, as shown in Figure 2(b)(i). As can be seen, the equilibrium state is

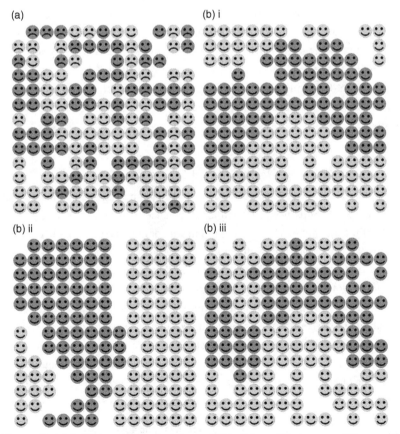

**Figure 2** (a) Initial conditions with $\sigma = 50\%$, (b) equilibrium conditions with (i) $\sigma = 50\%$, (ii) $\sigma = 66\%$, (iii) $\sigma = 33\%$

segregation between dark grey and light grey individuals, *caused by* the micro-level actions of individuals.

But what if we vary $\sigma$ to a higher number, say 66 per cent? If we do, the initial locations of individuals will be the same, but specific individuals now may be unhappy in their initial location (as they are subject to a higher threshold of similarity). If we allow this model to run, the equilibrium, as shown in Figure 2(b)(ii), still exhibits segregation with a more pronounced boundary between light grey and dark grey individuals. This is an expected result: with a higher threshold above 50 per cent, we would expect segregation to occur, as each individual wants to be in a local majority, and there is a clear driver of macro-level segregation.

The remarkable result from this model, however, appears when we lower the threshold $\sigma$ to below 50 per cent, say 33 per cent. This means that each individual is happy to be in a local minority. And not just any minority: they are happy to be outnumbered two-to-one by individuals of a different political affiliation. Intuitively, we would expect that in such a tolerant population, segregation would not occur. However, the results shown in Figure 2(b)(iii) demonstrate otherwise: there is *still* segregation between light grey and dark grey individuals, even in a seemingly tolerant population.

This agent-based model and other similar models exhibit *emergent* behavior, which is one of the characterizing features of complex systems, discussed below.

## 1.2 Complexity Science

The antecedents of agent-based models in strategic management can be traced back to the methods used in complexity science. Complexity science is the study of the interactions between individual actors in a system. While complex adaptive systems have been studied generally without specific applications in mind (Miller and Page 2007), Anderson, in the special issue of *Organization Science* devoted to complexity (Anderson 1999; Anderson *et al.* 1999), produces a review of the use of complexity science in organization science and breaks down the key elements of complex adaptive systems models into the following concepts: agents with schemata, self-organizing networks sustained by importing energy, co-evolution to the edge of chaos and recombination and system evolution. These concepts, however, are not novel in other academic fields. Indeed, in the preface to the special issue Lewin (1999:215) notes:

> [M]any of these ideas are not new. However, they do not simply represent old wine in new bottles ... this reframing gives me reason to believe that complexity science has much more to recommend to organization science.

Simon's definition – now more than half a century old (Simon 1962:468) – passes the test of time:

> [B]y a complex system, I mean one made up of a large number of parts that interact in a nonsimple way. In such a system, the whole is more than the sum of its parts.

We are relatively early in the journey of exploration of complexity science, particularly within strategic management. While the *NK* literature introduced in Section 3.1 has dominated agent-based modelling within organization and managerial science, we should not assume that this is the only model worthy of investigation: it is not, and there is scope for many more models to be brought into the domain of strategic management.

Bonabeau (2002) sets out the benefits of agent-based modelling as capturing emergent phenomena, providing a natural description of a system and being flexible. And it is the first concept, that of emergence, where agent-based modelling comes into its own. Emergence is a macro-level phenomenon brought about by the micro-level interaction of its constituent parts. In the preface to his book *Micromotives and Macrobehavior*, Schelling (1978) relates an anecdote in which, when he was giving a large public lecture, the first thirteen rows of an otherwise filled auditorium were left empty. When he asked why the seating had been arranged in this way, he was told it hadn't been: the individuals had apparently conspired to leave a gap at the front, their individual actions at the micro level combining into a noticeable effect at the macro/system level – in short, emergent behaviour. Schelling (1978:13) also makes the pertinent observation that to understand specific behaviours in this case is not to develop a specific understanding of, say, auditorium management, but rather the exact opposite: these emergent phenomena go far beyond individual realizations and are something much more fundamental. They involve:

> a kind of analysis that is characteristic of a large part of the social sciences, especially the more theoretical part. That kind of analysis explores the relation between the behavior characteristics of the *individuals* who comprise some social aggregate, and the characteristics of the *aggregate*.

Emergent behaviour can be found in a wide range of social and natural systems, for example, the flocking of birds, which can be modelled by the micro-level interactions of individual birds; the growth of crystals; convection; and the growth of cities.

The study of complex systems is inherently cross-disciplinary, exemplified by transdisciplinary research institutions such as the Santa Fe Institute (Dillon 2001), as the beauty of the study of complex systems is that the classes of problem that can be studied are not – or should not be – confined to the individual discipline being studied. In the case of strategic management, the class of problem is general in nature. The notion of sustainable competitive advantage, for example, can be thought of as a general concept, with parallels seen in the competition between species and within groups in the animal kingdom – where individuals aim to maximize not their performance but their 'fitness' – as well as in the self-organization of chemical reactions demonstrating cyclical behaviour. We should be ready to embrace these different application areas where complexity science has shown its promise and not be afraid to import ideas into management merely because a case does not match exactly the area in which we find our specific strategic and business problem.

Garcia (2005:383) summarizes agent-based models as being useful in the following circumstances:

- Where both micro and macro levels are of interest;
- Where social systems can be described by 'what if' scenarios but not by differential equations;
- When emergent phenomena may be observed;
- When co-evolving systems interact in the same environment;
- When learning and adaptation occurs;
- When physical space and temporal space are of interest;
- When the population is heterogeneous or the topology of interactions is complex and heterogeneous (e.g. social networks).

Anderson (1999) sets out a direction of travel for complexity research applied to management, citing D'Aveni's (1994) notion that the environment in which firms reside is 'hypercompetitive', explained by Anderson (1999:228) as 'nonlinearity lead[ing] both to unpredictable behavior and a rapid rate of change'. The new strategy for organizations under these conditions should therefore be to evolve temporary advantages faster than competitors (Brown and Eisenhardt 1998). Anderson also suggests that organizations can (a) attempt to alter 'the fitness landscape on which individual agents are trying to adapt, [while] strategists can change both the trajectory of emergent behavior and the diversity of behaviors in an organization's repertoire'; (b) 'reconfigure the organizational architecture within which agents adapt'; and (c) 'give executives guidelines to follow in evolving networks of agents'.

Agent-based models have now been widely used in other areas of management including innovation diffusion (Garcia and Jager 2011; Stummer *et al.* 2015), complexities in markets (Gilbert *et al.* 2007), entrepreneurship (McMullen and Dimov 2013), supply chains (Chang *et al.* 2008; Julka 2002; Kaihara 2003; Swaminathan 2007), and artificial financial markets (LeBaron 2000, 2006; Farmer and Foley 2009). They also are employed in marketing, diffusion of information and product adoption, retail location choice, inter-firm relationships and in the choice of marketing mix (Rand 2014), to name but a few more areas.

Traditional economists view the world as moving towards equilibrium or as at equilibrium – or at least as being able to *be* in equilibrium. There is a growing corpus of alternative economics, however, that shows the importance of diverging from the traditional views, and there have been calls for the use of natural science models within management by means of agent-based models (Robertson and Caldart 2008).

Holland and Miller (1991:365) describe complex adaptive systems (CAS) by defining complexity:

> [S]uch a system is complex in a special sense: (i) It consists of a network of interacting agents (processes, elements); (ii) it exhibits a dynamic, aggregate behavior that emerges from the individual activities of the agents; and (iii) its aggregate behavior can be described without a detailed knowledge of the behavior of the individual agents. An agent in such a system is *adaptive* if it satisfies an additional pair of criteria: the actions of the agent in its environment can be assigned a value (performance, utility, payoff, fitness, or the like); and the agent behaves so as to increase this value over time.

They go on:

> [A]ny given level can usually be described in terms of local niches that can be exploited by particular adaptations. The niches are various, so it is rare that any given agent can exploit all of them, as rare as finding a universal competitor in a tropical forest. Moreover, niches are continually created by new adaptations.

Allen *et al.* (2007) contrast economic general equilibrium theory with complexity science. They observe that economic theory can assume that equilibrium is the outcome of knowledge of a system by firms, as opposed to complexity science, where little needs to be known about the system as a whole.

Note that the definition of complexity has changed since the organizational ecology definitions of the 1980s (Hannan and Freeman 1984:162):

> [A]lthough the term complexity is used frequently in the literature to refer to the numbers of subunits or to the relative sizes of subunits, we use the term to refer to patterns of links among subunits. Following Simon (1962), we identify a simple structure with a hierarchical set of links ... 'nature loves a hierarchy'.

whereas Simon (1962) highlights the *decomposability* of social systems, a topic to which we shall return later in the context of *NK* models.

## 1.3 Tipping Effects, Cascades, Contagion, and Emergence

Schelling (1973) builds on the game-theoretical prisoners' dilemma and differentiates between *externalities*, the fact that the payoff of an individual depends on the choice of the other player, and *internalities*, the effect of the individual's payoff on their own choice.

Schelling (1973:385) notes that in the prisoners' dilemma game, the internality and the externality are opposed, and the externality outweighs the internality. Schelling then extends the prisoners' dilemma to multiple players, with a parameter $k$ being the number of players out of $n$ players in a multiple-player game that play dominated choices (those that make the dominated choices are better off than those that do not). Schelling then demonstrates the effect of $k$ by using four payoff matrices (these payoff matrices defaulting to the standard two-player payoff matrices when $k = n / 2$). Although these are not explicitly modelled as such, they are in fact multi-agent prisoners' dilemma models:

> [T]he literature on externalities has mostly to do with how much of a good or a bad should be produced, consumed, or allowed. Here I consider only the interdependence of choices to do or not to do, to join or not to join, to stay or to leave, to vote yes or no, to conform or not to conform to some agreement or rule or restriction. Joining a disciplined, self-restraining coalition, or staying out and doing what's natural is a binary choice. (Schelling 1973:382)

Schelling's concept of tipping (Schelling 1971a, 1971b, 1973, 1978) has been extended within sociology by Granovetter (1978) who developed Schelling's ideas of thresholds, while Macy (1991) built on that work, which later was popularized by Gladwell (2000).

Delre *et al.* (2007) studies the timing of new promotions from the perspective of the ability of a networked group of agents to spread an innovation (whether a technology or a product) across the network until all (or a significant percentage) of incumbents adopt the innovation as introduced, all building on the Bass diffusion model (Bass 1969). Delre *et al.* (2007) model the spread of a product across a fixed network of individuals. This is really a transition model from not-adopted to adopted on a fixed network and therefore is on the boundary of agent-based models and network models. A range of promotion strategies are modelled, comparing targeted versus mass promotion. This model is then extended by van Eck *et al.* (2011).

In order to capture the strategic management agent-based literature, the author has performed a systematic PRISMA analysis of the literature (Moher *et al.*, 2009; Vrabel, 2015) following the methodology of Utomo *et al.* (2017). Details are shown in the Appendix.

## 2 Antecedents: the World of Agent-Based Models

Where should we start? The possible range of antecedents to agent-based strategizing is huge:

> all aspects of organization that are relevant to adaptation ... mean[ing] ... that one could legitimately discuss everything that has been written about collective systems of all kinds. (Mintzberg *et al.* 1998:7 after Starbuck 1965:468)

But start somewhere we must. In this section, we review economic models, systems models, organizational ecology and fitness landscapes. These have been the underpinnings of current, and can be the underpinnings of future agent-based models for strategic management.

### 2.1 Economic Models

Tesfatsion (2002, 2006, 2017) summarizes the use of agent-based models in economics, along with Tesfatsion and Judd (2006). Schelling (1978:23) makes an interesting observation about economics:

> [T]wo hundred years ago Adam Smith characterized the system as one that worked as if some unseen hand brought about the coordination ... What [economists] do is to infer, from what they take to be the behavior characteristics of people, some of the characteristics of the system as a whole, and deduce some evaluative conclusions.

Bylund (2015) develops an agent-based model of Williamson's Transaction Cost Economics (Coase 1937; Williamson 1981) where firm formation is simulated, which has similarities with Axtell's (2001) work on the formation of firms resulting in the Zipf distribution of firm size. Holland and Miller (1991) introduced the notion of 'artificial adaptive agents in economic theory'.

### 2.2 Systems Models

The study of systems applied to management can be traced back to cybernetics, the study of 'the scientific study of control and communication in the animal and the machine' (Wiener 1948) introduced into management by Beer (1959). 'The first-order responses to experience are what Cyert and March (1963) called "problemistic search" and what Steinbruner (1974) characterized as "cybernetic"' (Levinthal and March 1981:309), defined by Simon (1962:467) as follows:

> the ideas that go by the name of cybernetics constitute, if not a theory, at least a point of view that has been proving fruitful over a wide range of

applications. It has been useful to look at the behaviour of adaptive systems in terms of the concepts of feedback and homeostasis, and to analyze adaptiveness in terms of the theory of selective information.

While different disciplines took general systems theory and made it specific – such as systems biology, systems ecology, systems engineering, systems psychology, etc. – its use within management has been taken up by the study of System Dynamics (SD).

System Dynamics is the study of how systems evolve, modelled through the concepts of stocks and flows, with feedback loops with delays and non-linear interactions. These concepts were introduced into management by Forrester (1961), with many attempts to include this methodology in mainstream strategic management (Cosenz and Noto 2016). Early SD research concentrated on strategy formulation and strategy support systems (Morecroft 1984, 1988) and the later popularization of systems thinking by Senge (1990) concentrated on organizational learning (Senge and Sterman 1992). The concept of the accumulation of a stock of assets has been brought into mainstream strategic management by Dietrikx and Cool (1989) to counter the resource-based view conceptualization of the acquisition of resources in strategic factor markets.

## 2.3 Organizational Ecology

Hannan and Freeman (1977, 1989), Hannan and Carroll (1992) and Carroll and Hannan (2000) introduce the concept of organizational ecology as an 'alternative to the dominant adaption perspective' (Hannan and Freeman 1977:929), making the distinction between selection and adaptation:

> [A]daptive learning for individuals usually consists of selection among behavioural responses. Adaptation for a population involves selection among types of members.

As we shall see later in this Element, adaptive learning for individual firms, albeit in a noncompetitive environment, is well covered in the *NK* literature.

Hannan and Freeman (1977:932) criticize economists' general equilibrium theory:

> [O]ne of the most difficult issues in contemporary economics concerns general equilibria. If one can find an optimal strategy for some individual buyer or seller in a competitive market, it does not necessarily follow that there is a general equilibrium once all players start trading ... until such a treatment is established we should not presume that a course of action that is adaptive for a single organization facing some challenging environment will be adaptive for many competing organizations adopting a similar strategy.

They take the following view (1977:939) on optimization of firms in a competitive environment:

> Consideration of optimization raises two issues: who is optimizing, and what is being optimized? It is quite commonly held, as in the theory of the firm, that organizational decision makers optimize profit over sets of organizational actions. From a population ecology perspective, it is the environment which optimizes.

Winter (1964) develops a theory of entry and exit of firms and a theory of 'natural selection' showing that individual rationality and market or environmental rationality do not usually lead to the same optima.

Hannan and Freeman (1977) develop the Lotka-Volterra (Lotka 1920, 1925; Volterra 1926) equations for competing populations (as opposed to the Lotka-Volterra equations for predator–prey interactions). This is a rich area for further research using agent-based as opposed to equation-based models.

The Lotka-Volterra model of competing populations can be described with the following formulae:

$$\frac{dN_1}{dt} = r_1 N_1 \left( \frac{k_1 - N_1 - \alpha_{12} N_2}{k_1} \right)$$

$$\frac{dN_2}{dt} = r_2 N_2 \left( \frac{k_2 - N_2 - \alpha_{21} N_1}{k_2} \right)$$

where the coefficients $\alpha_{12}$ and $\alpha_{21}$ are the competition coefficients – the effect that population 2 has on population 1, and the effect that population 1 has on population 2, respectively. These populations are denoted by $N_1$ and $N_2$, with $r_1$ and $r_2$ denoting the growth rates of the population in the absence of competition from the opposing population.

In order to visualize the dynamics of the populations, we can plot $N_1$ and $N_2$ against time as shown in Figure 3. Also shown is the population when there is no competition, which reduces to the logistic equation:

$$\frac{dN}{dt} = rN \left( \frac{k - N}{k} \right)$$

The parameters used in Figure 3 are $r = r_1 = r_2 = 0.1$; $k = 1$, $k_1 = 0.2$, $k_2 = 0.8$; $\alpha_{12} = \alpha_{21} = 0.1$; $dt = 0.5$; and $N_{1, t = 0} = 0.8$, $N_{2, t = 0} = 0.2$. In the absence of competition, the population reaches asymptotically its carrying capacity, $k$, whereas in the competitive Lotka-Volterra model, these equilibria are affected by the coefficients of competition $\alpha_{12}$ and $\alpha_{21}$ as well as the initial populations $N_{1, t = 0}$ and $N_{2, t = 0}$.

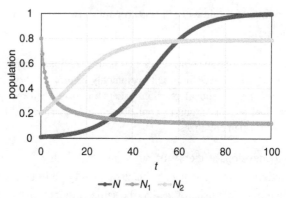

**Figure 3** Competitive Lotka-Volterra dynamics: $N_1$ and $N_2$ are competing populations. Also shown is $N$, the population in the absence of competition.


Hannan and Freeman (1977:942) show that populations are stable only if $1 \, / \, \alpha_{21} < k_2 \, / \, k_1 < 1 \, / \, \alpha_{12}$. This can be extended to competition between two populations where competition is generalized to be between *N populations* as follows:

$$\frac{dX_i}{dt} = r_i X_i \left( 1 - \frac{\sum_{j=1}^{N} \alpha_{ij} X_j}{k_i} \right)$$

where the populations and growth rates are vectors and the matrix of alphas, **A**, is the 'community matrix' whose elements are competition coefficients, which determine how much each population is affected by the other. This area of organizational ecology has not been as popular as niche width theory and density dependence and offers a way of building research for the future, building on the agent-based modelling of Lotka-Volterra modelling of predator–prey systems from system dynamics models to agent-based models (see Robertson 2019, Wilenksy and Reisman 1999, and Goel *et al.* 1971 for a review of the Lotka-Volterra models; Carroll (1984) gives an account of how they are used in organizational sociology).

One of the most prevalent parts of Hannan and Freeman's general theory of organizational ecology (Hannan and Freeman 1977:947) is their niche theory (as opposed to the above competition theory) where firms occupy specific locations:

> [T]he (realized) niche of a population is defined as that area in constraint space (the space whose dimensions are levels of resources etc.) in which the population outcompetes all other local populations. The niche, then, consists of all those combinations of resource levels at which the population can survive and reproduce itself.

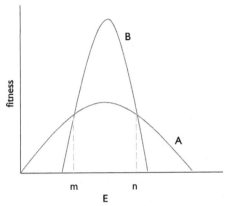

**Figure 4** Fitness functions for specialists and generalists (after Hannan and Freeman 1977:947)

We can see the similarity to the *NK* model in that fitness is a measurement of success of a population (as opposed to individual firms).

In Figure 4 (after Hannan and Freeman 1977:947), the fitness of two populations – generalists (A in the diagram, occupying a broad niches) and specialists (B in the diagram occupying a narrow niche) – are displayed as a function of the single environmental dimension, E.

Organizational populations are selected for or against based on the environment. Generalists are more able to adapt, having excess capacity: this allows firms to develop organizational slack (Penrose 1959; Cyert and March 1963), which is costly. In stable environments, generalists are outcompeted by specialists. In Figure 1, if the environmental variation remains within the interval [*m, n*], then generalists will be selected against; and conversely, if the environment is only occasionally within the interval, generalists will be favoured.

Other notions explored by Hannan and Freeman are density dependence and legitimation, age dependence and the liability of newness, inefficiencies of aging, liability of obsolescence and structural inertia (by means of internal factors such as sunk costs, culture and history; and external factors such as barriers to entry and legitimacy).

One of the limitations of organizational ecology is fitness, following Darwin's (1859) notion of natural selection or the 'survival of the fittest' (Spencer 1864). The notion of fitness can be related to either *survival* or reproductive success, which means 'endowed with phenotypic characteristics which improve the chances of survival and reproduction', and this does not immediately translate into the notions of competitive advantage, where *relative* fitness is sought rather than merely *not dying*.

The potential for organizational ecology within strategic management (Baum *et al.* 2006) has been elucidated, but still finds itself mainly discussed within organizational rather than strategic literature.

## 2.4 Biological Models and Fitness Landscapes: Rugged and Smooth Landscapes

A key way of modelling competitive situations is to conceive of an *N*-dimensional space, where the position in each of these dimensions is a strategic decision. This can be binary, 0 or 1, where the decision is either 'yes' or 'no', or it can be considered continuous, as in where we should position ourselves in geographical space or product characteristics space (Lancaster 1966). In more recent work, product space (Hildalgo *et al.* 2007) has been characterized by a network representation, where, looking at the overlap of exports and imports from countries, a distance measure can be made of the distance between individual products (a threshold is used to make the network less dense).

The original conceptualization of fitness landscapes came from the work of Sewall Wright (1932) in evolutionary biology. This is a mapping of position to fitness. For a one-dimensional choice, this would be a *two*-dimensional graph of location to fitness, or a profit function in economics, where the location can be chosen to maximize this profit. For a two-dimensional choice, for example the choice of where to locate in a geographical space, such as where to locate a firm in a town, a *three*-dimensional *landscape* can be generated.

Wright (1932:358) sets out the notion of fitness landscapes as follows:

> [I]n a rugged field of this character, selection will easily carry the species to the nearest peak, but there may be innumerable other peaks which are surrounded by 'valleys'. The problem of evolution as I see it is that of a mechanism by which the species may continually find its way from lower to higher peaks in such a field. In order that this may occur, there must be some trial and error mechanism on a grand scale by which the species may explore the region surrounding the small portion of the field which it occupies. To evolve, the species must not be under strict control of natural selection. Is there such a trial and error mechanism?

The role of strategy, therefore, is to produce that mechanism by which firms move around the fitness landscape in order to gain and maintain profitability. But the concept of competitive advantage is not so straightforward in these models, as *competition* is not present in at least the *NK* model, a topic which we shall turn to later in this Element.

Optimization on the fitness landscape can be thought of as maximizing fitness; or another way round is to think of minimizing energy (if the landscape is inverted so that maxima become minima).

It is relatively difficult to obtain a copy of the *NK(C)* model code (Vidgen and Padget 2009). And when you look at earlier models such as Levinthal's (1981) paper, even though the code is available in the paper itself, the online version of the paper is difficult to read, and the specific version of the language in which the code was created – believed to be Dartmouth BASIC – makes replication and extension of these models difficult; but see the Sendero project (Padget *et al.* 2008; Fioretti 2018) for versions of the *NK* computer code.

The landscape modelling technique has been developed by a series of authors from the *NK* model (see below, including Levinthal 1997, Levinthal and Warglien 1999, Rivkin and Siggelkow 2003, Gavetti and Levinthal 2000) and other models (McKelvey 1999, Fleming and Sorenson 2001).

The landscape model is a mapping between firm decisions and the payoffs that these decisions create. Most models assume that these models are static and that there is no effect of competition, which is a weakness of this approach. The general idea of this modelling conceptualization is that firms or organizations should aim to move to a position that is high on the performance landscape and sustain that position.

Siggelkow and Levinthal (2003:652) refer to this as a 'performance landscape':

> A performance landscape is a mapping of all possible sets of a firm's choices onto performance values (such as a profitability measure). If a firm's set of choices is described by a vector of $N$ choices, then the performance landscape consists of $N$ dimensions depicting the firm's alternatives along each dimension and an $(N + 1)$th dimension depicting the performance associated with each vector of $N$ choices.

Within the *NK* model, however, choices are binary: they can be either off or on. However, in depictions of performance landscapes (e.g., Siggelkow and Levinthal 2003:652), the choices are considered continuous. For if choices are binary, the decision 'landscape' is in fact the values on the vertices of an *N*-dimensional Boolean cube.

Landscape ruggedness is seen as an important factor when determining which search strategies should be used: Siggelkow and Levinthal (2003:652) state that the 'degree of interaction among a set of choices affects the ruggedness of the performance landscape (Kauffman 1993)'. This is true for the *NK* model but is not necessarily true for other performance landscape constructs.

Smoothness or ruggedness (Rivkin 2000) of a performance landscape can be defined as the number of local peaks – i.e., if moving locally from the current location in any direction does not result in performance gains.

## 3 Into the Strategic Literature

A fundamental question that has been attempted to be answered using agent-based models is Levinthal and March's (1981) dichotomy of whether firms should explore new territory or exploit the territory that they already occupy. Levinthal and March's paper includes as an appendix the computer code that gives the results shown in the paper – in some ways a precursor to the agent-based approach that would be, and indeed is used today, with the focus now on the *NK* model of search (later, Levinthal and March (1993) introduced the concept of the myopia of learning).

Levinthal and March's (1981) model of adaptive search and technological change uses a firm's search for new technologies through search, and the organizational learning that takes place as a result of the implementation of new technologies that are discovered as a result of that search. Notably, their work does not include competition between firms. Levinthal and March's (1981:308) model uses three components of firm behavior: the adaption of search strategies, the improvement of search competences, and the adaptation of aspirations.

> [W]e treat research and development or other forms of search as equivalent to drawing from a distribution of search outcomes ... the expected result of a draw is a function of the distribution of technological opportunities associated with a particular model of search and a particular technology.

Levinthal and March's model assumes that organizations set a performance target $G_t$ for each time period, which is modified on the basis of performance experience as follows:

$$G_t = b_1 P_{t-1} + (1 - b_1) G_{t-1}$$

so that the new target $G_t$ is an exponentially weighted moving average of past performance.

The motivation behind this is that if the performance target is greater than actual performance, organizations will search for solutions to this problem. Conversely, if performance exceeds the target, then organizational slack (being the difference between the potential performance of an organization and actual performance) accumulates.

Search costs are included in the model: refinement search cost, $R_t$ (of making an existing technology more efficient), and innovation search cost, $I_t$ (of finding a new improved technology):

$$P_t = (1 + a_t)T_{*,t} - R_t - I_t$$

The technology of the firm at time $t$, $T_{*,t}$, is the maximum of technological outcomes from the two search processes (refinement and innovation) and the technology of the previous period. But the previous period's technology changes at a constant rate $b_2$, where the value of $b_2$ determines whether the technology decays ($b_2 < 1$), remains the same ($b_2 = 0$), or improves ($b_2 > 1$), so:

$$T_{*,t} = \max\left(T_{r,t}, T_{i,t}, b_2 T_{*,t-1}\right)$$

In such a way, the organization searches on this technology space, but may not always find the best technology, instead finding $T_{i,t}$ the best technology discovered through innovation search during period $t$. Organizational search is performed by sampling some number of opportunities and then implementing the best if that technology exceeds the existing technology. Organizations may instead choose to refine their current technology. While this is not an agent-based model, it does create the notion of search over simple performance functions, which is developed in the later *NK* models.

## 3.1 The *NK* Model

The *NK* model was originally introduced in evolutionary biology by Kauffman (Kauffman 1993; Kauffman and Levin 1987; Kauffman and Weinberger 1989): The *NK* model defines the fitness of a piece of a chromosome. The chromosome is modeled as a string of genes, each in a position along a line. These genes can be expressed or not expressed, on or off. These positions – on or off – are called alleles A whose state is A = {0,1}. The fitness of the chromosome is computed as the summation on the component fitness of each element making up that chromosome. The elements can take a value of 0 (switched off) or 1 (switched on) and therefore are described as a Boolean (i.e., binary, 0 or 1) string.

Even though Kauffman first introduced the *NK* model as a theoretical evolutionary biology model, it was previously introduced as a physics spin glass model in an earlier paper (Kauffman 1984).

The rationale is that the model is that a 'tunably rugged' landscape can be created from just two parameters: $N$, the number of elements in the string, and $K$, the connections between the $N$ elements. This has a basis in the physicists' spin glass models. Spin glass models include the concept of frustration (Anderson 1988, Stein 2016) as $K$ increases. While spin glass models are used to *minimize* energy, we use them in the *NK* model to *maximize* fitness.

An element string is shown below:

| 0 | 1 | 1 | 1 |
|---|---|---|---|

In the simple model (where $K = 0$, which means there are no epistatic links) there is a simple relationship between whether the nucleotide is on or off (0 or 1) and the contribution to fitness, $f_i$, of that element:

| $f_1$ | $f_2$ | $f_3$ | $f_N$ |
|-------|-------|-------|-------|

where the fitness contribution $f_i$ is between 0 and 1.

The fitness, $F$, of the chromosome is simply the average of the fitness contributions $f_i$:

$$F = \frac{1}{N}\sum_{i=1}^{N} f_i$$

In the model above (where $N = 4$), $F = (f_1 + f_2 + f_3 + f_4) / 4$ so that if the contribution of a nucleotide with value 0 is, say, 0.2, and the value of a nucleotide with value 1 is 0.3, the mapping from the binary variable to the fitness contribution is random, for example:

$f_i = 0 \rightarrow 0.2$

$f_i = 1 \rightarrow 0.3$

making the fitness contributions:

| $f_1 = 0.2$ | $f_2 = 0.3$ | $f_3 = 0.3$ | $f_4 = 0.3$ |
|-------------|-------------|-------------|-------------|

so that

$$F = (1/N).(f_1 + f_2 + f_3 + f_4) = (0.2 + 0.3 + 0.3 + 0.3)/4 = 0.275$$

We can create a fitness *landscape* by calculating the fitness of each possible chromosome made of $N$ nucleotides. For $N = 4$, the number of contributions is $2 \times 2 \times 2 \times 2 = 2^N$.

In the case where $K = 0$, we can calculate the possible combinations and place these on an $N$-dimensional cube as follows:

| Nucleotide | | | Fitness Contribution | | | Fitness |
|---|---|---|---|---|---|---|
| 1 | 2 | 3 | $f_1$ | $f_2$ | $f_3$ | $F = \frac{1}{N}\sum_{i=1}^{N} f_i$ |
| 0 | 0 | 0 | 0.2 | 0.2 | 0.2 | 0.20 |
| 0 | 0 | 1 | 0.2 | 0.2 | 0.3 | 0.23 |
| 0 | 1 | 0 | 0.2 | 0.3 | 0.2 | 0.23 |
| 0 | 1 | 1 | 0.2 | 0.3 | 0.3 | 0.27 |
| 1 | 0 | 0 | 0.3 | 0.2 | 0.2 | 0.23 |

(cont.)

| Nucleotide | | | Fitness Contribution | | | Fitness |
| 1 | 2 | 3 | $f_1$ | $f_2$ | $f_3$ | $F = \frac{1}{N}\sum_{i=1}^{N} f_i$ |
|---|---|---|---|---|---|---|
| 1 | 0 | 1 | 0.3 | 0.2 | 0.3 | 0.27 |
| 1 | 1 | 0 | 0.3 | 0.3 | 0.2 | 0.27 |
| 1 | 1 | 1 | 0.3 | 0.3 | 0.3 | 0.30 |

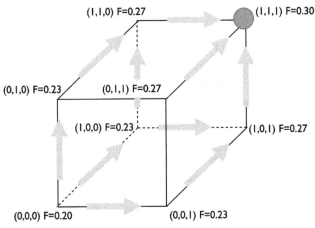

**Figure 5** Boolean hypercube fitness landscape

which can be represented on a Boolean hypercube as shown in Figure 5.

In this diagram, each vertex exhibits a fitness value. The red arrows show the attractors. So, for example, if we start at location (0, 0, 0) and follow a hill-climbing algorithm where you search locally to determine if there is a position that holds a greater fitness, and then move there and keep doing so until you are at a maximum fitness value, you will always reach the location represented by the purple circle (1, 1, 1) – this is the maximum fitness on the fitness landscape. And in the case of $K = 0$, there is only one maximum which is a global maximum (in that you will not be trapped in a suboptimal local peak). This is a relatively trivial model, and we need to introduce complexity – interactions between the elements of the system – in order to investigate the full extent of the *NK* model.

However, to make the fitness landscape more interesting and 'tunably rugged', we can introduce *epistasis*. This is modelled by the parameter $K$ ($0 \le K \le N-1$), the number of interactions with other elements. The interaction tables are randomly assigned, for example:

$$f_{00} \rightarrow 0.3$$
$$f_{01} \rightarrow 0.2$$

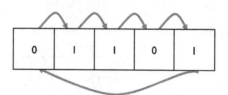

**Figure 6** *NK* model: $N = 5$, $K = 1$

$f_{10} \rightarrow 0.7$

$f_{11} \rightarrow 0.4$

These interactions can be randomly wired or systematically wired (where the fitness will be adjusted by the fitness of your immediate neighbour(s)).

Note that in Figure 6, the connections are with neighbouring elements and that the first and final elements are seen as connected. This topology is the same as the alleles being arranged in a circle. However, the results are robust to these connections being with random elements instead of with immediate neighbours (Kauffman 1993).

As an aside, parallels can be made with small-world networks where there is random rewiring of neighbouring elements. It would be an interesting area of future research to see if the rewiring from $K = 1$ in the circular state (as above) to a Watts and Strogatz (1998) random rewriting to a small-world network would make a difference in the results.

By increasing the parameter $K$, the 'ruggedness' of the landscape increases from a single-peaked 'Fujiyama' landscape to a multi-peaked 'badlands' landscape (Kauffman and Weinberger 1989).

The properties of *NK* landscapes are as follows (Orponen 2007):

- At $K = 0$, there is a unique global optimum, which is easily found by hill climbing (where comparison is made to immediate neighbouring vertices in the Boolean hypercube);
- At $1 \leq K \leq N - 1$: for $K = 1$, a global optimum can be found (in polynomial time) and for $K \geq 2$, global optimization is NP complete;
- $K = N - 1$: neighbouring genotypes are totally uncorrelated with the following statistics: the probability that a particular location is a local optimum is equal to the probability that the location has the highest fitness within its neighbours, whose probability is $1 / (N + 1)$; and the expected number of (local) optima is $2N / (N + 1)$.

Kauffman (1984:145) sets out the *NK* model as follows:

> [I]n its simplest form, a binary (Boolean) automaton is a deterministic dynamical system consisting of $N$ elements, or nodes, each capable of two values (activities, spins) 1 or 0. Nodes receive inputs from nodes in ways which may be geometrically simple, e.g. one, two or higher dimensional lattices with nearest neighbor interactions, and with all couplings

symmetrical; or complex, e.g. the nodes may be connected at random with one another by arrows denoting oriented asymmetric coupling such as model neural or genetic regulatory interactions. Since the elements are binary, the deterministic dynamical behavior of each element must be given by one of the possible $2^N$ Boolean functions of its $K$ inputs, specifying its next value, 1 or 0, for each of the $2^K$ combinations of values of its $K$ inputs.

Extensions to *NK* model include the *NK(C)* model (Kauffman 1993) applied to management by $K$ being split into two parameters: $K_W$ (the interdependencies within each business unit) and $K_B$ (the degree of interdependencies between business units) (Caldart and Ricart 2007).

Extensions to *NK* model include a pseudo-*NK* model (Valente 2014) where variables are modelled on real-value variables as opposed to Boolean values in the *NK* model. Valente (2014) notes a number of criticisms of the *NK* model:

- The use of binary variables
- Randomness to generate the landscapes
- Difficulty in its implementation and use

## 3.2 The *NK* Model: Applications and Framing of Strategic Problems

The *NK* model is the most researched agent-based model within management and strategy. It has built up an impressive series of papers after being introduced into the management literature by Levinthal (1997) and extended in the series of papers set out below.

### Levinthal (1997) – Adaptation on Rugged Landscapes

Levinthal's model creates an *NK* fitness landscape modelling the $N$ attributes of the organization. Organizations can then search and therefore adapt firstly by local search, where organizations examine the landscape locations at immediately neighbouring positions (where one of the $N$ entities is switched from 0 to 1 or vice versa).

Organizations then traverse the fitness landscape. Organizations, however, do not optimize in two respects. Firstly, they search locally, which may mean they become trapped in local (as opposed to global) optima; and secondly, they do not perform a 'greedy' search (one that appears to be the best choice at that time, thereby following the steepest slope) – this is the difference between 'simple hill climbing' and 'steepest ascent hill climbing'.

The concept of local search has been anchored in the strategy literature and discussed by Stuart and Podolny (1996) and Rosenkopf and Nerkar (2001) and builds on the work of March and Simon (1958) and Nelson and Winter (1982).

One of the limitations in using a hill-climbing algorithm is that global maxima are not always obtained, and therefore alternative methods such as stochastic hill climbing, random walks and simulated annealing methods can be used.

Levinthal (1997) uses an alternative method of search to overcome this: that of 'long jumps'. In this way, all $N$ attributes of the organization are changed at the same time so that the organization finds itself in a completely new location in $N$-dimensional (set at $N = 10$ in the model) Boolean space, which they compare to Tushman and Romanelli's (1985) conceptualization of 'reorientation'. In this 'innovative search', organizations choose the new location if the fitness value is greater than the existing fitness.

The steps in the simulation are as follows:

The fitness landscape is created, where each location in the $N$-dimensional Boolean space is ascribed a fitness. The fitness is calculated where each combination of alleles (e.g., 000, 001, 010, 011, 100 ... 111) is assigned for $K = 2$.

Next, a population of 100 organizations is created with random attributes, and taking random positions on the fixed fitness landscape.

The following loop is repeated:

1. A determination is made as to which organizations from the previous period survive.
2. Surviving organizations engage in both local and distant (long jump) search; organizations that find a preferential location adopt that organizational form.
3. Organizations are created to replace those that did not survive from the previous period, with the number of organizations kept constant at 100.

Levinthal finds that basins of attraction exist wherein organizations reduce to a few organizational forms; there is path-dependent adaptation (in that the history of the organization matters).

In order to model a changing environment, the model is rerun where halfway through the simulation at $t = 25$, the fitness landscape was respecified. With higher levels of $K$, local adaption is not an effective response to changing fitness landscapes.

Levinthal (1997:938) offers the following suggestion for future research:

> [T]he model does not address issues of population dynamics and niche-based competition. An important extension of this work would be to incorporate such features into the model structure.

We shall refer back to this in our agenda for the future of agent-based modelling.

### *Levinthal and Warglien (1999) – Landscape Design: Designing for Local Action in Complex Worlds*

Levinthal and Warglien (1999) emphasize the use of self-organization and local action, contrasting this to system approaches within the tradition of engineering control and design. They build on Kauffman and Weinberger's (1989:211) work defining adaptive evolution as follows:

> [A]daptive evolution is, to a large extent, a complex combinatorial optimiza-
> tion process. Such processes can be characterized as 'uphill walks' on rugged
> fitness landscapes.

The Levinthal and Warglien work emphasizes the fact that organizations can in fact *design* the landscape in which they operate by reducing interdependencies that lead to stable and predictable behaviors, or alternatively they can increase interdependencies by introducing cross-functional teams. There is therefore an opportunity to control – via landscape design – the tradeoff between ability to explore greater configurations and the expense of the coordination costs.

'Robust' organizational design is defined as a design with low interdependence between the elements of a system. Levinthal and Warglien assert that such robust design is desirable when it is not clear where the best solution is located (by way of the landscape being smooth and therefore a landscape designer being reasonably confident that the best solution will be found).

Levinthal and Warglien then introduce as a possible route for extension to their model Kauffman's (1994) $NK(C)$ model, where the new parameter $C$ indicates the number of the $N$ elements that are linked *across* entities (in this case, organizations), in contrast with the parameter $K$, which indicates inter-dependencies *within* an individual entity. The $NK(C)$ model – extension to the $NK$ model – is discussed within the management literature by Caldart and Oliveira (2010).

The concept of *coadaptation* between entities (for example, firm relations with customers or suppliers) is introduced (Levinthal and Warglien 1999:352):

> [T]raditional ideas of marketing strategy are premised on notions of product
> positioning (Kotler 1997). The 'landscape' for the firm consists of a position-
> ing map, with attributes on the axes and the density of consumers' ideal
> product or preference contours determining the topography of the landscape.
> The challenge of positioning is then to identify peaks that are not already
> crowded by competing products. We suggest the possibility of 'interactive
> marketing'. The landscape need not be fixed, but there may be interactions
> between customers' preferences and practices on one side and product
> features on the other side. As a result, there is some coevolution of offerings
> and preferences such that, over time, there is an increasing degree of inter-
> dependence between the product and consumer.

This opens up a rich avenue for future research, which we shall return to in the concluding paragraphs of this Element.

## McKelvey (1999) – Avoiding Complexity Catastrophe in Co-evolutionary Pockets: Strategies for Rugged Landscapes

McKelvey (1999) uses the results from Kauffman's (1993) work on the $NK(C)$ model to go further into the results from organizational co-evolution. McKelvey focuses on *complexity catastrophes* where organizations may be trapped on local (rather than global) optima and are on the 'edge of chaos' or the 'edge of catastrophe'. McKelvey (1999:308) highlights Kauffman's findings from his $NK(C)$ model:

> [A]s Kauffman has designed the *NK[C]* model, $K$ acts as a force toward increased complexity and complexity catastrophe whereas $C$ acts as a force away from catastrophe, that is, internal complexity leads to complexity catastrophe but external complexity leads away from catastrophe.

The findings that McKelvey uses are – applying the Kauffman findings to management – that firms should keep their internal value chain interdependencies, $K$, and their external interdependencies, $C$, to levels below their competitors.

## Rivkin (2000) – Imitation of Complex Strategies

Rivkin (2000) models several different strategies on a fixed $NK$ landscape to imitate strategies of a benchmarked firm.

A highpoint of the $NK$ landscape is first determined by the maximum fitness of 100 exploratory searches (note, this is not necessarily the global outcome in his latter 2001 paper). Imitator firms are then let loose on the landscape and are allowed to search for higher fitness. These imitative heuristics are as follows:

(a) *incremental improvement*, where firms consider all alternatives where they flip $M$ of their $N$ elements, and move to a new location if the fitness is greater than the current fitness (it is not clearly defined whether these are hill climbing or maximally hill climbing);

(b) *follow the leader imitation*, where firms attempt to reconfigure towards the benchmark firm at $s^*$. $J$ of $N$ decisions are adjusted to match the benchmark firm's choice, with the probability of it being matched correctly being $\theta \leq 1$.

(c) a hybrid search where a firm jumps towards the leader as in (b) above, and then moves uphill in (a).

Rivkin (2000) finds that firms that try to replicate a benchmark firm often will fail due to small errors in the configuration of their $N$ elements.

### Rivkin (2001) – Reproducing Knowledge: Replication without Imitation at Moderate Complexity

Rivkin (2001) builds on the *NK* model and posits that the complexity of a system can drive a 'wedge' between the ease of imitation and the ease of replication, where complexity is defined by the *NK* parameters of the number of elements *N* and the interactions between those elements *K*.

Rivkin extends the *NK* model by fixing a *NK* landscape in the normal way but divides firms that search this landscape into two types: replicators – 'R Firms' that are released close to the highest point on the landscape, and imitators – 'I Firms' that are released randomly on the landscape. The simulation is run and records the relative ability of imitators and replicators to find the optimal position on the landscape.

A second *NK* landscape is generated – with the same values of *N* and *K* but different fitness contributions – and the replicators and imitators are released onto this new landscape.

The results show that for values of $K = 0$, there is no advantage for being a replicator (as all hill-climbing strategies will find the global peak regardless of starting position). When *K* is raised slightly, the replicator benefits as the imitator gets stranded on local (i.e., nonglobal) peaks; and when *K* approaches *N*, the replicator's performance also is reduced as they also get stranded on local peaks.

### Rivkin and Siggelkow (2003) – Balancing Search and Stability: Interdependencies among Elements of Organizational Design

Rivkin and Siggelkow (2003) use the *NK* model to highlight the interdependencies between elements of organizational design. The results of their simulation show that there is a tradeoff between effort spent searching for better solutions and locking in to sets of decisions that may be suboptimal. They model this using a CEO, subordinate managers, and decisions between them. An incentive system is established where managers act for the firm as a whole for their own departmental interests.

Firms are allowed to roam the performance landscape. Although these firms are modelled as moving over the landscape concurrently (Rivkin and Siggelkow 2003:296), there is nothing in the model that takes into account the fact that many firms are roaming the landscape at the same time: there is no competition in the model, and if all firms started off at the same location, they would all reach the same end point. This is a significant limitation of the *NK* model – competition is not modelled.

In the Rivkin and Siggelkow model, the *NK* model is finessed by:

- The split of decisions in the firm's decision vector between subordinate managers. For instance, if there are $N = 6$ decisions, these may be allocated *ababbb* where *a* refers to decisions from manager a, and *b* refers to decisions under the control of manager b.
- Managers' search capability. This is modelled by a parameter, ALTSUB. If ALTSUB = 5, this means that the manager will search for five alternatives to the current decision part of the decision vector under their control. They search locally in that decisions where only one bit is flipped are exhausted before the decision where two bits are flipped is considered.
- Managers' incentive structure, using parameter Incent, with Incent being between 0 and 1. This weights the contributions between those under the manger's control and those outside. If INCENT = 0, the payoff computed by the manager will exclude those under the other manager's control; if INCENT = 1, this will include them.

The cognitive ability of the CEO is also modelled. The parameter ALTCEO takes into account whether a CEO rubberstamps the decisions of subordinates, or whether they consider the choices that they have been presented by subordinates.

### *Siggelkow and Levinthal (2003) – Temporarily Divide to Conquer: Centralized, Decentralized and Reintegrated Organizational Approaches to Exploration and Adaptation*

Siggelkow and Levinthal (2003) consider the change in environment, where the *NK* model is altered. The authors show that where a firm's activities are not 'decomposable' into independent, non-interacting subunits (contrasting with Ethiraj and Levinthal's (2004) work on modularity), neither centralized nor decentralized organizational structure leads to high performance. Instead, organizations need to take on a 'temporary decentralization with subsequent regeneration' where the organization un-forms and re-forms. As such, the organization explores possible solutions and then coordinates across its divisions. This links to March's (1991) debate as to exploration versus exploitation.

The difference between this and the standard *NK* model is that firms are exposed to a one-time environmental shock. Siggelkow and Levinthal (2003:657) model the effect of disruption on firms that are initially located at a global peak, causing the location of the global peak to change. In the case of $N = 6$, for example, there are $2^N$ possible locations. The environment is changed so that the location of the peak is moved. The ability of firms to find the location of the global peak is calculated. They find that 're-integrators' are more able to find global peaks compared to centralized firms, since the decentralized search causes the firms to escape from the 'basin of attraction' of a low peak.

### Gavetti, Levinthal, and Rivkin (2005) – Strategy Making in Novel and Complex Worlds: the Power of Analogy

Gavetti *et al.* (2005) use the *NK* model to show how firms can discover competitively advantageous positions that are both novel and complex. They find that local search is unlikely to lead to an advantageous position. In their work, they contest that analogizing managers choose a subset of industry characteristics that distinguish similar industries from different ones. When a new industry is faced, a familiar industry is seen as an analogy to the novel one. They develop a series of *NK* landscapes – analogies to their current landscapes where the degree of similarity can be controlled.

They divide strategies as follows:

(a) Local searchers who use hill climbing only and do not use analogy;
(b) Analogizers who use their strategy based on similar landscapes that they have previously experienced.

Gavetti *et al.* (2005) extend Kauffman's model by introducing a hierarchy of choices: $P$ high-level policy decisions, each of which comprises $D$ detailed choices. They also split $K$ into $K_w$, the probability of interdependency within the policy domain, and $K_b$, the interdependency between policy domains. Their simulations find that the power of analogy is strongest when interactions among decisions cross policy boundaries so that the underlying decision problem is not easily decomposed.

### Siggelkow and Rivkin (2006) – When Exploration Backfires: Unintended Consequences of Multilevel Organizational Search; and Rivkin and Siggelkow (2006) – Organizing to Strategize in the Face of Interactions: Preventing Premature Lock-In

Siggelkow and Rivkin (2006) extend the *NK* model by assuming that decisions are split between two department managers. This extends the Siggelkow and Rivkin (2003) model above and focuses on a parameter, ALT, the extent of explorative activity by lower-level managers who feed their decisions up to the CEO.

They find that when CEOs delegate decisions to lower-level managers, they may save time, but those lower-level managers may screen out opportunities that are seen not to be optimal *for the lower-level manager*. But when these are recombined at the CEO level, the *overall* optimal decision for the whole firm may not be available to the CEO, and hence overall firm performance may suffer.

### *Lenox, Rockart, and Lewin (2006) – Interdependency, Competition and the Distribution of Firm and Industry Profits*

Lenox *et al.* (2006) combine the *NK* model with a Cournot model of price competition. They map the cost/quality distribution from an *NK* model to competitive outcomes, which produces additional interdependencies between the *K* of the *NK* model and the price mechanism.

They find that industry profits (in the model) are affected by the level of *K* – interdependencies, which they term 'Potential for Interdependency among Activities', or PIA for short. This model is a first attempt at combining perfor-mance landscapes with a price dimension, although it does not explicitly model competition between firms but just the price being set as a result of a Cournot price-setting mechanism that determines the overall average (and therefore total) industry profit.

### *Gavetti, Helfat, and Marengo (2017) – Searching, Shaping and the Quest for Superior Performance*

Gavetti *et al.* (2017) use a modified *NK* model – the *NKES* model (described fully in Suzuki and Arita 2005) – where in addition to the *N* policy choices, there are additional *Z* policy dimensions, where, when a firm makes a change to these *Z* policy choices, the payoff function changes for *all* firms. There is a parameter $E$ ($0 \leq E \leq Z$), operating in a similar way as *K* operates to *N*. Therefore, the firm has a choice between *searching* over the performance landscape or *shaping* by concentrating on the *Z* policy dimensions.

## 3.3 Other Rugged Landscape Models

Chang and Harrington (2000:1428) use a model of firms searching over a rugged landscape defined as the 'space of store practices':

> [A] store's performance (profit) depends on how its current set of operating practices matches up with what is desired by its consumers. New ideas represent a new point in store practice space, and associated with that new point is a level of profit.

Chang and Harrington (2000) build on the organizational learning models of 'boundedly rational agents experimenting with new ideas and making piecewise improvements (Cohen 1981, Levinthal and March 1981, Nelson and Winter 1982)'. However, Chang and Harrington (2000:1429) use a different formulation for the adaptive search mechanism to answer the question: what is the optimal degree of centralization versus decentraliza-tion within a firm?

Each store is in a distinct market and has a set of $N$ practices such that store $i$'s operation in any given period is fully described by a vector, $z^i \equiv (z^i_1, z^i_2, \ldots, z^i_N)$, where $z^i_j$ is store $i$'s practice for the $j$th dimension of its operation and $z^i_j \in \{1, \ldots, R\}$ for all $i \in \{1, \ldots, M\}$, and $j \in \{1, \ldots, N\}$. Thus, there are $R$ feasible practices for each dimension and, at any point in time, a store is represented by a point in $\{1, \ldots, R\}^N$.

Conversely, all consumers in market $i$ shop at store $i$. Each consumer has an ideal set of store practices. Therefore, the interaction between firms and consumers characterizes the Profit Function. This opens up an interesting area for future research.

Carley and Svoboda (1996) model a performance surface where the surface is determined by a number of parameters $p_1 \ldots p_n$. They use a process of simulated annealing, borrowed from condensed matter physics and used in such problems as solving the travelling salesman time in polynomial time (Černý 1985), as a metaheuristic to search for the maximum of the performance surface – minimizing the 'energy' of a system by using this heuristic in a way that may produce the global maximum rather than a local maximum that would be found using a hill-climbing algorithm. This extended the 'ORGAHED' model in Carley and Lee (1998) where organizations are seen to fall into strategic traps when the performance landscape is dynamic.

Robertson (Robertson 2003; Robertson and Caldart 2009) introduces a model of customer and firm agents, whose combination presents a complex profit surface over which firms can move, endogenously deforming the landscape as they move. A menu of strategies is modelled, and the success of strategies under differing environmental conditions can be modelled.

## Product Space Creating the Landscape

Garcia (2005) show an agent-based model for the spread of an innovation, while the interaction between consumers and firms is modelled by Tay and Lusch (2005).

Allen *et al.* (2007) use a model of firms and potential customers where firms compete in 'strategy space' with two dimensions: percentage mark-up and quality; and consumers decide between products that are sold by the firms. This results in niches that are profitable for specific firms. They model four different strategies for firms: a 'Darwinian' strategy where there are no learning and random strategies; 'Old Strategy' where, if the profit is less than half the average, the percentage is reduced; 'Hill Climbing'; and a mixture of hill climbers and imitators. Moreover, they determine that the best strategy cannot be deduced from a game-theoretical approach.

## 3.4 Other Agent-Based Strategic Management Models

### *Intra-organizational Knowledge Sharing*

Wang *et al.* (2009) introduce a model of knowledge sharing within an organization, where employees are endowed with knowledge-sharing strategies that determine how they individually share information and, as a result, how information is shared in the organization. By allowing the firm to vary the incentives (positive or negative) for sharing information (outwardly or inwardly), results can be determined as to the percentage of individuals within the firm that contribute to knowledge sharing within the organization.

### *Threshold Models – No Social Influence: Individuals Respond to Community Parameter*

Miller *et al.* (2009) consider strategies for firms involved in online communities, where such communities are 'seeded' with product advocates, as opposed to attempting to control interactions within these communities. Miller *et al.* (2009:307) suggest that 'anonymity and aliases allow a firm's representatives to disguise their product endorsements as input from peers'. The model uses *thresholds* where individuals consider adoption of an opinion if expressed by a proportion of a community's members that exceed an individual's threshold level. These *cascades and tipping effects* are used as a mechanism for social contagion.

Miller *et al.*'s model uses a population of $n$ individuals who participate in $c$ equally sized online communities of initial size $n / c$. Individuals' preferences for a particular product are either negative (a value of $-1$), neutral (value 0) or positive (value $+1$). Individuals both give information to and receive information from the online community. As individuals post opinions with a fixed probability, the proportion of positive to negative opinions in the community changes. Agents can switch from positive to negative opinion or vice versa when the proportion of postings exhibiting the alternative view exceeds a threshold.

The strategic intervention is that firms have $a$ advocates, that they can decide to switch between alternative online communities ($a \ll n$), with the strategy objective of influencing preferences towards a favorable view of its product. The following strategies are modelled: *support the strong*, where advocates are allocated to communities according to the number of favorable postings about the product; *support the weak,* where advocates are allocated according to unfavorable postings about the product; and a *uniform strategy,* where advocates are allocated according to the sizes of the communities.

A fixed population (900 individuals) from a fixed number of communities (9) is modelled, with varying preferences across different communities. The model is run to consider the switching efficacy of carrying out the different strategies. Results are presented to show the favored strategy for different switching assumptions.

## 4 An Agenda for the Future

Neither the Levinthal and March (1981) model of adaptive organizational search nor the *NK* series of models includes competition. This is a significant limitation, and perhaps shows why these models were first introduced into the organizational theory rather than strategic management literature. There is therefore a large scope to include competitive models, perhaps from other domains, and to translate these into the strategic management literature. This review highlights the limitations and a research agenda for agent-based models within strategic management.

Agent-based models now find themselves in an ever-widening range of fields, some far away from strategic management. The introduction of evolutionary models, via organizational ecology, to the *NK* model, has been an archetype of how this is done well. But the range of agent-based models in social as well as natural sciences (Robertson and Caldart 2008) is largely untapped. There is therefore a roadmap to revitalizing what appear to be tired areas of strategic management that have been limited to the unavailability of data or the isomorphism that has crept into the literature. We set out below some areas for thought.

Going back to Levinthal and March (1981:307):

> [The model] does not consider the effects of competition, imitation, or other interaction among organizations. It explores some ways simple adaptation might lead to organizational change, and how that process might be complicated by the confusions of a changing and autonomous environment and by the interrelation of different adaptive processes.

## 4.1 Dynamic Feedback Models

Feedback and dynamics need to be incorporated into agent-based models if they are to be realistic representations of competitive environments (Robertson and Caldart 2009). Hill-climbing algorithms or other strategies can be modelled where there is feedback between the environment and the firm's strategy. While simple heuristics may work in a static environment, these same heuristics may not work when firms search over a *dynamic* rugged landscape. This is fine for where the landscape does not deform in the time to search. And how can firms determine the direction in which to travel without travelling to a new location? Firms cannot experiment within strategic management: a firm either takes a strategic move in strategic space, or it does not.

Unlike economic models, there is not the elegance of finding an equilibrium. But real-life situations are not deterministic: repeating the decisions that have been made in the past does not necessarily produce outcomes that are repeatable. And as such, the use of economic models may not be the most appropriate in strategic management.

## 4.2 Competitive Models

There is a rich opportunity for agent-based models to be used in competitive situations – something that so far has been only weakly taken up.

Opportunities lie in several areas such as competitive agent-based models, and competitive models from other social science and natural science disciplines. Complexity science still has an enormous opportunity within strategic management, and the tools and techniques of agent-based modelling are a prime example of where these can be studied.

There is also an opportunity to work with data (big or otherwise). Agent-based models up until now have been used largely as stand-alone worlds where firms are studied in controlled conditions (those of economics), on specific landscapes or in tightly controlled environments. However, if these tools are to make real advances, they need to be verified and validated against real-world data, and further iterations of the models made to take into account these advances in our understanding. This opens up rich opportunities for new research directions.

## 4.3 Turning Existing Analytical Models into Agent-Based Models

Economic models generally assume that equilibrium exists, or can exist, and that firms instantaneously switch between equilibria – a form of comparative statics rather than dynamics. However, the *path to equilibrium* is as important as the equilibrium itself. This is an area that can be studied in some depth and is a suggested area for future research. A rich source of existing models is found in the modelling libraries of agent-based modelling toolkits such as *NetLogo* and *RePast*. There are several agent-based modelling toolkits that allow agent-based models to be created ever faster (although coding is still required to develop models; see Robertson 2005). Several software packages are available for exploring agent-based modelling (Robertson 2005). NetLogo (Wilensky 1999) contains several models from other natural- and social-science domains.

A roadmap of how these models can be transferred to strategic management problems is set out below.

## 4.4 Agent-Based Models on Networks

Many of the agent-based models use strategies played out on fitness or performance landscapes, where firms are seeking high levels of fitness or performance. Another topology that can be explored is that of networks. In some ways, the NK model can be thought of as a Boolean *network* (albeit a very ordered one). But there exist many other network topologies – some of which are discussed in Robertson (2019) – which offer opportunities for future research.

Troutman *et al.* (2008) set out a model of language change where a social network exists over which two grammars or languages exist: individuals converse in either grammar A or language B. Neighbours of individuals then update their grammar according to update rules. In this way, mediated by the structure of the interpersonal social network, grammars spread across a social network. This builds on work by Watts (2002) on the spread of innovations through a network. And there is scope for coupling to existing models of percolation and self-organized criticality, such as the forest fire models (Bak *et al.* 1987; Bak and Chen 1991).

In a strategic context, such network models can be used to model the transferral of a standard across a customer (social) or company (inter-firm) network. Firms can then either work on changing the thresholds of individuals in the network by, for example, lock-in to the network, or disrupt the connectivity of the network, by, for example, targeting super-spreaders or nodes with a high centrality in order to actively encourage the transferral of the preferred standard (or conversely, disrupt the transferral of a competing standard).

There are similarities in topology between the random rewiring in network models such as Watts and Strogatz small-world networks and the interconnection parameter $K$ within $NK$ models. Integrating these two streams of research is an opportunity for future work.

Schelling (1971) attacks the same problem from a different perspective, that of whether individuals or individual firms are in a local minority. When individuals are surrounded by others who are of a different type (for example, political affiliation), they move to a different location. The results of this work show that there is segregation of individuals on the basis of political affiliation even if individuals are happy to be in a local minority.

Fang *et al.* (2014) build on Schelling's (1971) and Axelrod's (1997) model and apply a grid-based performance search, while Miller *et al.* (2009) use the concept of segregation in their models and use the concept of tipping points introduced by Schelling (1978) to show how a system – in this case, online communities – can, when crossing a certain threshold, change from one state to another.

## 4.5 Inter-species Populations and Inter-firm Competition

The organizational ecology literature does not consider the dynamics of the system. System dynamics models consider the population as a whole without considering the individual elements of the system. Wilensky and Reisman (1999, 2006) take a model of codependent populations and apply an agent-based perspective, generating qualitatively similar population dynamics but from the micro-level interactions of individual agents. Hannan and Freeman (1977) build on the Lotka-Volterra competitive model, which could be turned into an agent-based model, rather like the predator–prey model has been converted into an agent-based model in earlier work.

## 4.6 Punctuated Equilibrium Models, Isomorphism and the Spread of Norms

The Lotka-Volterra predator prey model of different species shows dynamics where what appears to be a steady equilibrium is punctuated by rebounds of populations. However, models such as Epstein's (2002) model of civil violence show punctuated equilibrium dynamics more clearly.

Epstein (2001) introduces a model of social norms (isomorphism) which could be used as a model to support DiMaggio and Powell's (1983) thesis of institutional isomorphism: 'constraining process that forces one unit in a population to resemble other units that face the same set of environmental conditions'. Epstein (2001:10) states:

> [I]n this model, then, agents learn how to behave (what norm to adopt), but they also learn *how much to think about* how to behave. How much they are thinking affects how they behave, which – given how others behave – affects how much they think. In short, there is *feedback* between the social (inter-agent) and internal (intra-agent) dynamics ... we are looking for the stylized facts regarding the spatio-temporal evolution of norms: local conformity, global diversity, and punctuated equilibria. (Young 1998)

There is still a wealth of ideas, concepts and techniques being developed in complexity science, modelled by agent-based models. We should ensure that we revisit the concepts introduced to us by early organizational researchers such as Simon (1962) and the early industrial organization or systems models (such as Hotelling 1929 and the Lotka-Volterra models) to see if we can reconceptualize these using agent-based modelling, a technique that I am sure would have been used if available to these researchers. The work of complexity institutes such as the Santa Fe Institute is on the cutting edge of completive and complex systems, albeit not in the specific domain of strategic management. If we do not interact with researchers in a transdisciplinary way, strategic management risks being left behind and not catching up to more forward-thinking economists. To go back to the quote from Herbert Simon (1962:467):

> [I]t may not be entirely vain, however, to search for common properties among diverse kinds of complex systems ... The ideas of feedback and information provide a frame of reference for viewing a wide range of situations, just as do the ideas of evolution, of relativism, of axiomatic method, and of operationalism.

This is the task for strategy researchers – and agent-based modelling is a vehicle to make transformative leaps in theory. I close this Element as I started: Strategic management, in line with other social science fields, is difficult. It is a subject that does not lend itself easily to experimentation, as the environment co-evolves at the same time in which specific strategies are being evaluated. Agent-based modelling offers an exciting opportunity to experiment where interactions between other firms and the complex environment can be modelled and robust strategies developed accordingly. The future for agent-based strategizing is bright.

# References

Allen, P. M., Strathern, M., and Baldwin, J. S. (2007) 'Complexity and the Limits to Learning', *Journal of Evolutionary Economics*, **17**(4), 401–31

Anderson, P. (1999) 'Complexity Theory and Organization Science', *Organization Science*, **10**(3), 216–32

Anderson, P. W. (1988) 'Spin Glass Hamiltonians: a Bridge between Biology, Statistical Mechanics and Computer Science, In: Pines, D. (Ed.) *Emerging Syntheses in Science*, pp. 17–20, Redwood City, CA: Addison-Wesley

Anderson, P., Meyer, A., Eisenhardt, K., Carley, K., and Pettigrew, A. (1999) 'Introduction to the Special Issue: Applications of Complexity Science to Organization Science', *Organization Science*, **10**(3), 233–6

Axelrod, R. (1997) *The Complexity of Cooperation: Agent-Based Models of Competition and Collaboration*, Princeton, NJ: Princeton University Press

Axelrod, R. and Tesfatsion, L. (2006) 'A Guide for Newcomers to Agent-Based Modeling in the Social Sciences', In: Tesfatsion, L. and Judd, K. L. (Eds.), *Handbook of Computational Economics: Agent-Based Computation in Economics*, New York, NY: North-Holland

Axtell, R. (2001) 'Zipf Distribution of U. S. Firm Sizes', *Science*, **293**, 1818–20

Bak, P. and Chen, K. (1991) 'Self-Organized Criticality', *Scientific American* **264**, 46–53

Bak, P., Tang, C., and Wiesenfeld, K. (1987) 'Self-Organized Criticality: an Explanation of $1/f$ Noise', *Physical Review Letters*, **59**(4), 381–4

Bass, F. M. (1969) 'A New Product Growth for Model Consumer Durables', *Management Science*, **15**(5), 215–27

Baum, J. A. C., Dobrev, S. D., and Van Witteloostuijn, A. (2006) *Ecology and Strategy*, Amsterdam: Elsevier

Beer, A. S. (1959) 'Cybernetics and Management', London: English Universities Press

Bonabeau, E. (2002) 'Agent-based Modeling: Methods and Techniques for Simulating Human Systems', *Proceedings of the National Academy of Sciences of the United States of America*, **99**(Supplement 3), 7280–7

Brown, S. L. and Eisenhardt, K. M. (1998) *Competing on the Edge: Strategy as Structured Chaos*, Boston, MA: Harvard Business School Press

Bylund, P. L. (2015) 'Signifying Williamson's Contribution to the Transaction Cost Approach: an Agent-Based Simulation of Coasean Transaction Costs and Specialization', *Journal of Management Studies*, **52**(1), 148–74

Caldart, A. A. and Oliveira, F. (2010) 'Analysing Industry Profitability: a "Complexity as Cause" Perspective', *European Management Journal*, **28**, 95–107

Caldart, A. A. and Ricart, J. E. (2007) 'Corporate Strategy: an Agent-Based Approach', *European Management Review*, **4**, 107–20

Carley, K. M. and Lee, J.-S. (1998) 'Dynamic Organizations: Organizational Adaptation in a Changing Environment', *Advances in Strategic Management*, **15**, 269–7

Carley, K. M. and Svoboda, D. M. (1996) 'Modeling Organizational Adaptation as a Simulated Annealing Process', *Sociological Methods and Research*, **25**(1), 138–68

Carroll, G. (1984) 'Organizational Ecology', *Annual Review of Sociology*, **10**(1), 71–93

Carroll, G. R. and Hannan, M. T. (2000) 'The Demography of Corporations and Industries', Princeton, NJ: Princeton University Press

Černý, V. (1985) 'Thermodynamical Approach to the Traveling Salesman Problem: an Efficient Simulation Algorithm', *Journal of Optimization Theory and Applications*, **45**, 41–51

Chang, M.-H. and Harrington, J. E. (1998) Organizational Structure and Firm Innovation in a Retail Chain', *Computational and Mathematical Organization Theory*', **3**(4), 267–88

Chang, M.-H. and Harrington, J. E. (2000) 'Centralization vs. Decentralization in a Multi- Unit Organization: a Computational Model of a Retail Chain as a Multi-Agent Adaptive System', *Management Science*, **46**(11), 1427–40

Chang, T.-H., Lee, J.-Y., and Chen, R.-H. (2008) 'The Effects of Customer Value on Loyalty and Profits in a Dynamic Competitive Market', *Computational Economics*, **32**, 317–39

Coase, R. (1937) 'The Nature of the Firm', *Economica*, **4**(16), 386–405

Cohen, M. D. (1981) 'The Power of Parallel Thinking', *Journal of Economic Behavior and Organization*, **2**(4), 285–306

Cosenz, F. and Noto, G. (2016) 'Applying System Dynamics Modelling to Strategic Management: a Literature Review', *Systems Research and Behavioral Science*, **33**(6), 703–41

Cyert, R. M. and March, J. G. (1963) *A Behavioral Theory of the Firm*, Englewood Cliffs, NJ: Prentice-Hall

Darwin, C. (1859) *On the Origin of Species by Means of Natural Selection, or the Preservation of Favoured Races in the Struggle for Life*, London: John Murray

D'Aveni, R. A. (1994) *Hypercompetition: Managing the Dynamics of Strategic Maneuvering*, New York, NY: Free Press

Delre, S. A., Jager, W., Bijmolt, T. H. A., and Janssen, M. A. (2007) 'Targeting and Timing Promotional Activities: an Agent-Based Model for the Takeoff of New Products', *Journal of Business Research*, **60**, 826–35

Dierickx, I. and Cool, K. (1989) 'Asset Stock Accumulation and Sustainability of Competitive Advantage', *Management Science*, **35**(12), 1504–11

Dillon, D. (2001) 'Review of the Santa Fe Institute: Institutional and Individual Qualities of Expert Interdisciplinary Work', Working Paper, Harvard Interdisciplinary Studies Project

DiMaggio, P. J. and Powell, W. (1983) 'The Iron Cage Revisited: Institutional Isomorphism and Collective Rationality in Organizational Fields', *American Sociological Review*, **48**, 147–60

Epstein, J. M. (1999) 'Agent-Based Computational Models and Generative Social Science', *Complexity*, **4**(5), 41–60

Epstein, J. M. (2001) 'Learning to Be Thoughtless: Social Norms and Individual Computation', *Computational Economics*, **18**, 9–24

Epstein, J. M. (2002) 'Modeling Civil Violence: an Agent-Based Computational Approach', *Proceedings of the National Academy of Sciences of the United States of America*, **99**(3), 7243–50

Epstein, J. M. and Axtell, R. L. (1996) *Growing Artificial Societies: Social Science from the Bottom Up*, Cambridge, MA: MIT Press

Ethiraj, S. K. and Levinthal, D. (2004) 'Modularity and Innovation in Complex Systems', *Management Science*, **50**(2), 59–173

Farmer, J. D. and Foley, D. (2009) 'The Economy Needs Agent-Based Modelling', *Nature*, **460**, 685–6

Federal Trade Commission (2009) 'Guides Concerning Use of Endorsements and Testimonials in Advertising', 16 C. F. R. (Code of Federal Regulations) § 255

Fioretti, G. (2018) 'Computer Code for the NK Model', www.cs.unibo.it/~fioretti/CODE/NK/, accessed June 2018

Fleming, L. and Sorenson, O. (2001) 'Technology as a Complex Adaptive System: Evidence from Patent Data', *Research Policy*, 30(7), 1019–1039

Forrester, J. W. (1961) *Industrial Dynamics*, Cambridge, MA: MIT Press

Garcia, R. (2005) 'Uses of Agent-Based Modeling in Innovation/New Product Development Research', *Journal of Product Innovation Management*, **22**, 380–98

Garcia, R. and Jager, W. (2011) 'From the Special Issue Editors: Agent-Based Modeling of Innovation Diffusion', *Journal of Product Innovation Management*, **28**, 148–51

Garcia, R. and Rummel, P. (2004) 'Netlogo, Exploratron/Exploitation Dilemma in Innovation Model', http://ccl.northwestern.edu/netlogo/models/community/EXPLORE%20VS%20EXP OLTE, accessed June 2018

Gardner, M. (1970) 'Mathematical Games – The Fantastic Combinations of John Conway's New Solitaire Game "Life"', *Scientific American*, **223**, 120–3

Gavetti, G., Helfat, C. E., and Marengo, L. (2017) 'Searching, Shaping, and the Quest for Superior Performance', *Strategy Science*, **2**(3), 194–209

Gavetti, G. and Levinthal, D. A. (2000) 'Looking Forward and Looking Backward: Cognitive and Experiential Search', *Administrative Science Quarterly*, **45**, 113–37

Gavetti, G., Levinthal, D. A., and Rivkin, J. W. (2005) 'Strategy Making in Novel and Complex Worlds: The Power of Analogy', *Strategic Management Journal*, **26**, 691–712

Gilbert, N. (2008) 'Agent-Based Models', Thousand Oaks, CA: Sage

Gilbert, N., Jager, W., Deffuant, G., and Adjali, I. (2007) 'Complexities in Markets: Introduction to the Special Issue', *Journal of Business Research*, **60**(8), 813–5

Gilbert, N. and Troitzsch, K. (2005) *Simulation for the Social Scientist*, Maidenhead, UK: Open University Press

Gladwell, M. (2000) *The Tipping Point: How Little Things Can Make a Big Difference*, London: Little, Brown.

Goel, N. S., Maitra, S. C., and Montroll, E. W. (1971) 'On the Volterra and Other Nonlinear Models of Intereacting Populations', *Reviews of Modern Physics*, **43**, 231–76

Goldenberg, J., Libai, B., and Muller, E. (2010) 'The Chilling Effects of Network Externalities', *International Journal of Research in Marketing*, **27**, 4–15

Granovetter, M. (1978) 'Threshold Models of Collective Behavior', *American Journal of Sociology*, **83**(6), 1420–43

Hannan, M. T. and Carroll, G. R. (1992) *Dynamics of Organizational Populations*, New York, NY: Oxford University Press

Hannan, M. T. and Freeman, J. (1977) 'The Population Ecology of Organizations', *American Journal of Sociology*, **82**(5), 929–64

Hannan, M. T. and Freeman, J. (1984) 'Structural Inertia and Organizational Change', *American Sociological Review*, 49(2), 149–64

Hannan, M. T. and Freeman, J. (1989) *Organizational Ecology*, Cambridge, MA: Harvard University Press

Hildalgo, C. A., Klinger, B., Barabási, A.-L., and Hausmann, R. (2007) 'The Product Space Conditions in the Development of Nations', *Science*, **317**, 482–7

Holland, J. H. and Miller, J. H. (1991) 'Artificial Adaptive Agents in Economic Theory', *American Economic Review*, **81**(2), 365–70

Hotelling, H. (1929) 'Stability in Competition', *The Economic Journal*, **39**(153), 41–57

Julka, N., Srinivasan, R., and Karimi, I. (2002) 'Agent-Based Supply Chain Management – 1: Framework', *Computers and Chemical Engineering*, **26**, 1755–69

Kaihara, T. (2003) 'Multi-Agent Based Supply Chain Modelling with Dynamic Environment', *International Journal of Production Economics*, **85**, 263–9

Kauffman, S. A. (1984) 'Emergent Phenomena in Random Complex Phenomena', *Physica D*, 145–56

Kauffman, S. A. (1993) *The Origins of Order: Self-Organization and Selection in Evolution*, New York, NY: Oxford University Press

Kauffman, S. A. and Levin, S. (1987) 'Towards a General Theory of Adaptive Walks on Rugged Landscapes', *Journal of Theoretical Biology*, **128**, 11–45

Kauffman, S. A. and Weinberger, E. D. (1989) 'The *NK* Model of Rugged Fitness Landscapes and Its Application to Maturation in the Immune Response', *Journal of Theoretical Biology*, **141**, 211–45

Kotler, P. (1997) *Marketing Management*, New York, NY: Prentice-Hall

Lancaster, K. J. (1966) 'A New Approach to Consumer Theory', *The Journal of Political Economy*, 74(2), 132–157.

LeBaron, B. (2000) 'Agent-Based Computational Finance: Suggested Readings and Early Research', *Journal of Economic Dynamics and Control*, **24**(5–7), 679–702

LeBaron, B. (2006) 'Agent-Based Computational Finance', In: Tesfatsion, L. and Judd, K. L. (Eds.) *Handbook of Computational Economics*, 2, 1187–233

Lenox, M. J., Rockart, S. F., and Lewin, A. Y. (2006) 'Interdependency, Competition, and the Distribution of Firm and Industry Profits', *Management Science*, **52**(5), 757–72

Levinthal, D. A. (1997) 'Adaptation on Rugged Landscapes', *Management Science*, **43**, 934–50

Levinthal, D. A. and March, J. G. (1981) 'A Model of Adaptive Organizational Search', *Journal of Economic Behavior and Organization*, **2**(4), 307–33

Levinthal, D. A. and March, J. G. (1993) 'The Myopia of Learning', *Strategic Management Journal*, **14**, 95–112

Levinthal, D. A. and Warglien, M. (1999) 'Landscape Design: Designing for Local Action in Complex Worlds', *Organization Science*, **10**(3), 342–57

Lewin, A. Y. (1999) 'Application of Complexity Theory to Organization Science', *Organization Science*, **10**(3), 215

Lotka, A. J. (1920) 'Analytical Note on Certain Rhythmic Relations in Organic Systems', *Proc. Natl. Acad. Sci. U.S.A.*, **6**, 410–5

Lotka, A. J. (1925) *Elements of Physical Biology*, Baltimore, MD: Williams & Wilkins

Macy, M. W. (1991) 'Chains of Cooperation: Threshold Effects in Collective Action', *American Sociological Review*, **56**(6), 730–47

March, J. G. (1991) 'Exploration and Exploitation in Organizational Learning', *Organization Science*, **2**(1), 71–87

March, J. G. and Simon, H. (1958) *Organizations*, New York, NY: Wiley

McKelvey, B. (1999) 'Avoiding Complexity Catastrophe in Coevolutionary Pockets: Strategies for Rugged Landscapes', *Organization Science*, **10**(3), 294–321

McMullen, J. S. and Dimov, D. (2013) 'Time and Entrepreneurial Journey: The Problems and Promise of Studying Entrepreneurship as a Process', *Journal of Management Studies*, **50**(8), 1481–512

Midgley, D. F., Marks, R. E., and Cooper, L. C. (1997) 'Breeding Competitive Strategies', *Management Science*, **43**, 257–75

Miller, J. H. and Page, S. E. (2007) *Complex Adaptive Systems: An Introduction to Computational Models of Social Life*, Princeton, NJ: Princeton University Press

Miller, K. D., Fabian, F., and Lin, S.-J. (2009) 'Strategies for Online Communities', *Strategic Management Journal*, **30**(3), 305–22

Mintzberg, H., Ahlstrand, B., and Lampel, J. (1998) *Strategy Safari: A Guided Tour Through the Wilds of Strategic Management*, London: Prentice Hall

Moher, D., Liberati, A., Tetzlaff, J., Altman, D. G., and Group, P. (2009) 'Preferred Reporting Items for Systematic Reviews and Meta-Analyses: The PRISMA Statement, *PLoS Medicine*, **6**, e1000097

Morecroft, J. D. W. (1984) 'Strategy Support Models', *Strategic Management Journal*, **5**(3), 215–29

Morecroft, J. D. W. (1988) 'System Dynamics and Microworlds for Policymakers', *European Journal of Operational Research*, **35**, 301–20

Nelson, R. R. and Winter, S. G. (1982) 'An Evolutionary Theory of Economic Change', Cambridge, MA: Harvard University Press

North, M. J. and Macal, C. M. (2007) 'Managing Business Complexity: Discovering Strategic Solutions with Agent-Based Modeling and Simulation', Oxford: Oxford University Press

Orponen, P. (2007) 'Combinatorial Models and Stochastic Algorithms', Helsinki University of Technology Laboratory for Theoretical Computer Science, https://users.ics.aalto.fi/orponen/lectures/komsta_2007.pdf

Padget, J., Vidgen, R., Mitchell, J., Marshall, A., and Mellor, R. (2008) 'Sendero: An Extended, Agent-Based Implementation of Kauffman's NKCS Model', University of Bath Working Paper, https://wiki.bath.ac.uk/display/sendero/NKC, accessed June 2018

Penrose, E. T. (1959) *The Theory of the Growth of the Firm*, New York, NY: Wiley

Rand, W. (2014) 'The Future Applications of Agent-Based Modeling in Marketing', In: Moutinho, L., Bigne, E., and Manrai, A. K. (Eds.) *The Routledge Companion to the Future of Marketing*, London: Routledge

Rivkin, J. W. (2000) 'Imitation of Complex Strategies', *Management Science*, **46**(6), 824–44

Rivkin, J. W. (2001) 'Reproducing Knowledge: Replication without Imitation at Moderate Complexity', *Organization Science*, **12**(3), 274–93

Rivkin, J. W. and Siggelkow, N. (2003) 'Balancing Search and Stability: Interdependencies among Elements of Organizational Design', *Management Science*, **49**(3), 290–311

Rivkin, J. W. and Siggelkow, N. (2006) 'Organizing to Strategize in the Face of Interactions: Preventing Premature Lock-in', *Long Range Planning*, **39**, 591–614

Robertson, D. A. (2003) 'Agent-Based Models of a Banking Network as an Example of a Turbulent Environment: the Deliberate vs. Emergent Strategy Debate Revisited', *Emergence*, **5**(2), 56–71

Robertson, D. A. (2005) 'Agent-Based Modeling Toolkits: NetLogo, RePast, and Swarm', *Academy of Management Learning and Education*, **4**(4), 525–7

Robertson, D. A. (2019) 'Spatial Transmission Models: a Taxonomy and Framework', *Risk Analysis*, **39**(1), 225–43

Robertson, D. A. and Caldart, A. A. (2008) 'Natural Science Models in Management: Opportunities and Challenges', *Emergence: Complexity & Organization*, **10**(2), 61–75

Robertson, D. A. and Caldart, A. A. (2009) *The Dynamics of Strategy*, Oxford: Oxford University Press

Robinson, S. (2004) *Simulation: The Practice of Model Development and Use*, Chichester: John Wiley & Sons

Rosenkopf, L. and Nerkar, A. (2001) 'Beyond Local Search: Boundary-Spanning, Exploration, and Impact in the Optical Disk Industry', *Strategic Management Journal*, **22**(4), 287–306

Schelling, T. C. (1969) 'Models of Segregation', *American Economic Review*, **59**(2), 488–93

Schelling, T. C. (1971a) 'Dynamic Models of Segregation', *Journal of Mathematical Sociology*, 1, 143–86

Schelling, T. C. (1971b) 'On the Ecology of Micromotives', *The Public Interest*, 25, 61–98

Schelling, T. C. (1973) 'Hockey Helmets, Concealed Weapons, and Daylight Saving: a Study of Binary Choices with Externalities', *Journal of Conflict Resolution*, **17**(3), 381–428

Schelling, T. C. (1978) *Micromotives and Macrobehavior*, Norton

Senge, P. (1990) *The Fifth Discipline: The Art & Practice of the Learning Organization*, New York, NY: Doubleday

Senge, P. and Sterman, J. D. (1992) 'Systems Thinking and Organizational Learning: Acting Locally and Thinking Globally in the Organization of the Future', *European Journal of Operational Research*, **59**, 137–50

Shiozawa, Y. (2016) 'A Guided Tour of the Backside of Agent-Based Simulation', In: Kita, H., Taniguchi, K., and Nakajima, Y. (Eds.) *Realistic Simulation of Financial Markets: Analyzing Market Behaviors by the Third Mode of Science*, Economics and Social Complexity Science, **4**, Japan: Springer

Siggelkow, N. and Levinthal, D. A. (2003) 'Temporarily Divide to Conquer: Centralized, Decentralized, and Reintegrated Organizational Approaches to Exploration and Adaptation', *Organization Science*, **14**(6), 650–69

Siggelkow, N. and Rivkin, J. W. (2006) 'When Exploration Backfires: Unintended Consequences of Multilevel Organizational Search', *Academy of Management Journal*, **49**(4), 779–95

Simon, H. A. (1947) *Administrative Behavior: a Study of Decision-Making Processes in Administrative Organization*, 1st ed., New York, NY: Macmillan

Simon, H. A. (1962) 'The Architecture of Complexity', *Proceedings of the American Philosophical Society*, **106**, 67–82

Simon, H. A. (1996) *The Sciences of the Artificial*, 3rd ed., Cambridge, MA: MIT Press

Simon, H. A. (1997) *Administrative Behavior: a Study of Decision-Making Processes in Administrative Organizations*, 4th ed., New York, NY: The Free Press

Spencer, H. (1864) *Principles of Biology*, London: William and Norgate

Starbuck, W. (1965) 'Organizational Growth and Development', In: March, J. G. (Ed.) *Handbook of Organizations*, Chicago, IL: Rand-McNally

Stein, D. L. (2016) 'Frustration and Fluctuations in Systems with Quenched Disorder', In: *PWA90: A Lifetime of Emergence*, Chandra, P., Coleman, P., Kotliar, G., Ong, N. P., Stein, D. L. and Yu, C. (Eds.), Singapore: World Scientific, pp. 169–86

Steinbruner, J. D. (1974) *The Cybernetic Theory of Decision: New Dimensions of Political Analysis*, Princeton, NJ: Princeton University Press

Stuart, T. E. and Podolny, J. M. (1996) 'Local Search and the Evolution of Technological Capabilities', *Strategic Management Journal*, **17**, 21–38

Stummer, C., Kiesling, E., Gunther, M., and Vetschera, R. (2015) 'Innovation Diffusion of Repeat Purchase Products in a Competitive Market: an Agent-Based Simulation Approach', *European Journal of Operational Research*, **245**, 157–67

Suzuki, R. and Arita, T. (2005) 'How Niche Construction Can Guide Coevolution', In: Capcarrere, M. S., Freitas, A. A., Bentley, P. J., Johnson, C. G., and Timmis, J. (Eds.) *Advances in Artificial Life: 8th European Conference, ECAL 2005*, Canterbury, UK; Berlin: Springer-Verlag

Swaminathan, J. M., Smith, S. F., and Sadeh, N. M. (2007) 'Modeling Supply Chain Dynamics: a Multiagent Approach', *Decision Sciences*, **29**(3), 607–32

Tay, N. S. P. and Lusch, R. F. (2005) 'A Preliminary Test of Hunt's General Theory of Competition: Using Artificial Adaptive Agents to Study Complex and Ill-Defined Environments', *Journal of Business Research*, **58**(9), 1155–68

Tesfatsion, L. (2002), 'Agent-Based Computational Economics: Growing Economies from the Bottom Up', *Artificial Life*, **8**(1), 55–82

Tesfatsion, L. (2006) 'Agent-Based Computational Economics: a Constructive Approach to Economic Theory', In: Tesfatsion, L. and Judd, K. L. (Eds.), *Handbook of Computational Economics*, Volume 2: Agent-Based Computational Economics, Elsevier

Tesfatsion, L. (2017) 'Modeling Economic Systems as Locally-Constructive Sequential Games', *Journal of Economic Methodology*, **24**(4), 1–26

Tesfatsion, L. and Judd, K. L. (Eds.) (2006) *Handbook of Computational Economics*, Volume 2: Agent-Based Computational Economics, Elsevier

Troutman, C., Clark, B., and Goldrick, M. (2008) 'Social Networks and Intraspeaker Variation During Periods of Language Change', *University of Pennsylvania Working Papers in Linguistics*, **14**(1), Article 25

Tushman, M. and Romanelli, E. (1985) 'Organizational Evolution: a Metamorphosis Model of Convergence and Reorientation', In: Cummings, L. and Staw, B. (Eds.) *Research in Organizational Behavior*, **7**, 171–222

Utomo, D. S., Onggo, B. S., and Eldridge, S. (2017) 'Applications of Agent-Based Modeling and Simulation in the Agri-Food Chains', *European Journal of Operational Research*, **269**, 794–805

Valente, M. (2014) 'An NK-Like Model for Complexity', *Journal of Evolutionary Economics*, **24**(1), 107–34

Van Eck, P. S., Jager, W., and Leeflang, P. S. H. (2011) 'Opinion Leaders' Role in Innovation Diffusion: a Simulation Study', *Journal of Product Innovation Management*, **28**, 187–203

Vidgen, R. and Padget, J. (2009) 'Sendero: an Extended, Agent-Based Implementation of Kauffman's NKCS Model', *Journal of Artificial Societies and Social Simulation*, **12**(4), 8

Volterra, V. (1926) 'Variazioni e fluttuazioni del numero d'individui in specie animali conviventi', *Mem. Acad. Lincei Roma*, **2**, 31–113

Von Neumann, J. (1966) *Theory of Self-Reproducing Automata*, Burks, A. W. (Ed.), Champaign, IL: University of Illinois Press

Vrabel, M. (2015) 'Preferred Reporting Items for Systematic Reviews and Meta- Analyses', *Oncology Nursing Forum*, 552–4

Wang, J., Gwebu, K., Shanker, M., and Troutt, M. D. (2009) 'An Application of Agent- Based Simulation to Knowledge Sharing', *Decision Support Systems*, **46**, 532–41

Watts, D. (2002) 'A Simple Model of Global Cascades on Random Networks', *Proceedings of the National Academy of Sciences of the USA*, **99**, 5766–71

Watts, D. J. and Strogatz, S. H. (1998) 'Collective Dynamics of "Small-World" Networks', *Nature*, **393**(6684), 440–2

Wiener, N. (1948) *Cybernetics, or Control and Communication in the Animal and the Machine*, Cambridge, MA: MIT Press

Wilensky, U. (1999) *NetLogo*, Evanston, IL: Center for Connected Learning and Computer-Based Modeling, Northwestern University

Wilensky, U. and Reisman, K. (1999) 'ConnectedScience: Learning Biology through Constructing and Testing Computational Theories – an Embodied Modeling Approach', *International Journal of Complex Systems*, 234, pp. 1–12

Wilensky, U. and Reisman, K. (2006) Thinking Like a Wolf, a Sheep or a Firefly: Learning Biology through Constructing and Testing Computational Theories – an Embodied Modeling Approach, *Cognition and Instruction*, **24**(2), 171–209

Williamson, O. E. (1981) 'The Economics of Organization: the Transaction Cost Approach', *American Journal of Sociology*, **87**(3), 548–77

Winter, S. G. (1964) 'Economic "Natural Selection" and the Theory of the Firm', *Yale Economic Essays*, **4**, 224–72

Woodridge, M. and Jennings, N. R. (1995) 'Intelligent Agents: Theory and Practice', *Knowledge Engineering Review*, **10**, 115–52

Wright, S. (1932) 'The Roles of Mutation, Inbreeding, Crossbreeding, and Selection in Evolution', *Proceedings of the Sixth International Congress on Genetics*, 355–66

Young, H. P. (1998) *Individual Strategy and Social Structure*, Princeton, NJ: Princeton University Press

# Appendix: PRISMA Methodology

The following criteria were used to search *Web of Science*:
TS=("agent based" OR "multi agent") AND TS=("strategic management" OR "strategy") AND WC=("business" OR "management")

  and the following criteria were used to search *Scopus*:
TITLE-ABS-KEY (("agent based" OR "multi agent") AND ("strategic management" OR "strategy")) AND (LIMIT-TO (SUBJAREA, "BUSI "))

| Search | Search Field | Search Term | Web of Science | Scopus | Total |
|---|---|---|---|---|---|
| A | TS (Topic) | Agent Based | 24,565 | 37,772 | |
| B | TS | Multi Agent | 31,576 | 65,264 | |
| C = A OR B | | | 51,260 | 93,036 | |
| D | TS | Strategic Management | 9,525 | 10,336 | |
| E | TS | Strategy | 909,535 | 2,169,948 | |
| F = D OR E | | | 932,424 | 2,176,018 | |
| G | WS (Web of Science Category) | Business | 597,043 | 1,426,940 | |
| H | WS | Management | 682,995 | n/a | |
| J = G OR H | | | 1,108,956 | 1,426,940 | |
| K = C AND F AND J | | | 383 | 515 | 898 |

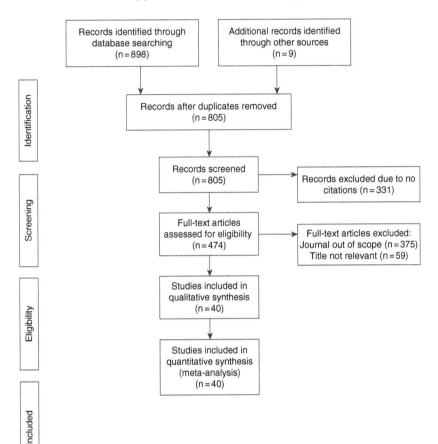

Cambridge Elements $\equiv$

# Business Strategy

## J.-C. Spender
*Rutgers Business School*

JC Spender is a visiting scholar at Rutgers Business School and a research Professor, Kozminski University. He has been active in the business strategy field since 1971 and is the author or co-author of seven books and numerous papers. His principal academic interest is in knowledge-based theories of the private sector firm, and managing them.

## About the Series
Business strategy's reach is vast, and important too since wherever there is business activity there is strategizing. As a field, strategy has a long history from medieval and colonial times to today's developed and developing economies. This series offers a place for interesting and illuminating research including industry and corporate studies, strategizing in service industries, the arts, the public sector, and the new forms of Internet-based commerce. It also covers today's expanding gamut of analytic techniques.

## Cambridge Elements ≡

# Business Strategy

## Elements in the Series

*Scenario Thinking: Infusing Planning with Foresight*
Brad MacKay and Peter McKiernan

*Agent-Based Strategizing*
Duncan A. Robertson

A full series listing is available at: www.cambridge.org/EBUS

CPSIA information can be obtained
at www.ICGtesting.com
Printed in the USA
LVHW031922211019
634872LV00014B/447/P